Quotes from Bar

author of The Jelly Bean Principle

"The Empire State Building wasn't built in a day, but the idea for it came in a minute."

"An entrepreneur's mind works 24/7."

"If your goal is too easy, your effort will be also."

"Instead of looking over your shoulder, turn around and face the situation."

"Brainstorm with your employees, don't brainwash."

"The only thing worse than having another birthday is not having one."

"When you lose a customer to a competitor, don't blame them, blame yourself."

"A gift you can give to everyone is your smile."

"The contrarian is the trend setter."

"Haste makes waste and you may have to clean it up."

"Every day can't be 72 degrees and sunny."

"When opportunity knocks, make sure someone is home."

"The most optimistic person you'll ever meet is an entrepreneur without any money."

OTHER BOOKS

BY BARRY THOMSEN

- When the Shit Hits the Fan: How to Keep Your Business Afloat for More Than a Year
- Save Your Business: 25 Common Business Threats and How to Avoid Them
- Chasing Success: The Street Smart Guide to Owning a Business
- Never Never Land: Bring that Customer Back (2010)

THE
JELLY BEAN
PRINCIPLE

THE

JELLY BEAN PRINCIPLE

105 WAYS TO STAND OUT FROM COMPETITORS

Barry Thomsen

Oak Tree Press   Taylorville, IL

Oak Tree Press books may be purchased for educational, business or sales promotional purposes. Contact Publisher for quantity discounts

First Edition, May 2009

Cover by MickADesign.com

ISBN 978-1-892343-59-8

LCCN 2001012345

DEDICATION

This book is dedicated to my wife, Sam Su,
who has inspired me to success.

INTRODUCTION

Starting a business is easy, Almost anyone can do it. It's happening everyday across America, over a million times a year. Serving customers and clients profitably is what it's all about. But attracting those customers that make a new business or mature one prosperous and feed growth is a whole different thing. A dime and a doorknob will keep you open for one day but how will you survive tomorrow, next week and next year? How will you pay the rent, fixed expenses, employees and maybe even yourself? How will you establish your dream of owning and operating a business that you can be proud of? You won't, without new and repeat customers continually buying from your business. And to get those valuable customers, you'll need to be unique and offer something no one else in your industry is offering the same way. That something is what your new or existing business is all about and why it will be successful. Some call it U.S.P. (unique selling proposition) but it's really how you *stand out* from your competitors. And most of your competitors will be looking for the same thing themselves.

Most types of businesses have competitors. It's just a fact of life. When people see a successful market, they jump in and try to grab part of it. It's sort of like a jar of jelly beans of all different colors and each one is a different competitor. Your business is just one of them and will get lost in the jar unless you find a way to stand out. Why should anyone pick you over all the other jelly beans? What makes you attract the customer when there are so many to choose from? You want to be their selected choice, not their random choice. That's what this book is all about.

You don't only have to be a new business to be searching for that product, quality level or service that makes you different, current and mature businesses need these ideas also. Innovation and uniqueness is a journey that never ends. It just turns and twists and searches for new territory — a road that takes you and your customer to places that you have never been before, a road that will show you concepts and ways of doing ordinary procedures in new and different ways. Even if it's only a small change that improves a product, service or a way of delivering it, the market will buy it if it's presented correctly. And reaching the target market that will be excited about your idea and buy it, is what this book is all about. It doesn't matter whether it's a 24/7 beauty salon, a come-to-you oil change, a laser printer with a two year color cartridge, or life-extending cancer drug, it has to be found and seen by the market it's intended to benefit. What good is a super idea that will benefit others if it sits in your garage or in a computer file? Who's going to find it there?

The Jelly Bean Principle is going to show you ways of getting your business and unique ideas in front of the people who will want to buy them. They may have been waiting for your new idea for a long time, so don't let them wait any longer. It would be great if we could all introduce our new products and services on prime time television but for most of us the cost is more than winning the lottery. And we could sell our product to a larger corporation who does have the resources but then they will get most of the profits if it's successful. You will only get a small part of the profits if the idea is not already proven as a commercial success. If you are planning to sell out later, wait until it has some success and your reward will be much greater. Look at companies like *You Tube,* that may only have been worth $10,000.00 when it started but sold for about $400 million after it became successful. For that kind of increase in value, it's worth the struggle to get it going first, *before* you sell out.

I remember when I was a boy I always liked to spend money. But since my allowance was $1.00 a week, I needed a job to be able to buy the things I wanted. When I was 10 ½ years old, I saw that the paper route in my neighborhood was suddenly available. The previous carrier had let it run down and lost many customers. The route only had about 30 customers, but you needed at least 50 to make good money. It was an afternoon paper, *Chicago's American* (no longer in business) so every day after school I delivered papers to the customers and stopped at the other houses to get new subscriptions. I told them they would get a dry, clean and on time paper every day. And they would get the latest news from earlier that day that wouldn't be in our competitor's paper, the *Chicago Tribune,* until the next day. I would be their paper boy and personally guaranteed excellent service every day.

The newspaper also had a special offer for new subscribers who signed up for at least 13 weeks of delivery. It was their choice of a kitchen clock or a set of steak knives. I think my approach was so sincere and convincing that for half the orders I never got to the free gift, they signed up before that. But since the newspaper expected to give them away, I told the distributor I needed one or the other for every new subscriber. My mother said she had enough clocks and steak knives so I took them to a nearby hardware store who bought them from me for $2 each. I eventually built that route to over 90 customers who received first-class service on sunny, rainy and snowy days. And my tips and Christmas gifts proved they were satisfied.

There are many ways to break into your customer's mind and buying habits and you'll see 100 or more in this book. It doesn't really matter if your business is retail, medical or business to business, you will need some way to open the market to your new product or idea. And you can't always rely on only one venue for promoting your idea, you will need several. What you think will be the big breakthrough may not work and what you're not sure of may be the one that opens all the doors. So look for as many marketing ideas that will pertain to your idea and try all that you can fit in your budget. Each person you are trying to reach or get to notice your company may find you in a different way. There is no sure-fire method that works for everyone. The best mode is through word-of-mouth but you must first reach the ones that will start it, and completely satisfy them.

Getting a new product, service or idea in front of the correct target market is not always easy and sometimes it just doesn't make it at all. Throwing more money at a losing marketing idea never works either. If it is not working, change it and try a different method that may work. Try thinking outside the (school) book and be an innovator, not a follower. I've been in small business marketing for years with my many businesses and I'm constantly surprised at something new that I've tried. You just never know what can make you a super success. So you must try and test as many ways that you can. Remember that this book is trying to direct you in the right marketing direction and you can modify any of the ideas here to adapt to your own situation. Be the jelly bean that stands out in the jar.

Keep in mind that everything you see here is not right for every business. Saying that, the outrageous or the unexpected can draw a lot of attention if done the right way. So don't eliminate anything just because it's never been done before. It just may work. I always smiled when someone said, "You can't do that. It will never work," and I was determined to prove them wrong. I may not have succeeded every time but enough to make it profitable. And seeing your business rise above all those pesky competitors out there is the greatest feeling of success. There are no textbook solutions to every marketing situation, only past performances. And like a horse race, the future is still to be determined, by you.

CONTENTS

1

GIVE THEM MORE

Who wouldn't want more than they think they paid for? That little extra that leaves a great impression on a patron, customer or client and brings them back again. It also makes them feel like they have to tell everyone they know. That something that they didn't expect and may have pleasantly surprised them. The bonus they received without paying any more for and was actually free. An unexpected reward for doing nothing more than being a customer. A show of appreciation by the retailer, vendor or salesperson that is rarely seen today. It's unexpected because it wasn't advertised or used to entice you to buy or order. Wow, this doesn't happen every day!

It really doesn't have to be a lot, an extra bagel in a dozen, 5 minutes more for a massage, an extra bone for your dog when you buy a roast, an upgraded hotel room or a call the next day from your doctor's office to see how you are. How often do we get these things; seldom or never? And how much does it really cost the seller to give them? Very little or nothing in most cases. It shows that you care for the people who are supporting you, your business and your employees. In return your customers will likely remember and be repeat customers when they need your products or services again. Don't forget the word-of-mouth advertising it creates.

So many people in today's business climate feel they barely get what they are paying for and maybe a little less. It really stands out when it happens the other way around because it's so rare. Large corporations seem to give you the minimum necessary and spend their money on massive advertising to entice you to buy. If they spent more on giving that *little extra*, customers would buy again without being reminded three times a day. That's why a smaller business can get a decent market share without spending those advertising megabucks that they don't have anyway. Big business knows how to advertise but rarely how to over-serve their customers. Employees are taught a routine and most of them stop there.

I remember a time that I was going on a golf trip and while packing the night before my favorite pair of slacks were still in the cleaner's basket. I forgot to take them in and now I couldn't pack them. I went to my usual dry cleaners when they opened at 7 AM and asked if they could be done by 11 AM so I could put them in my suitcase. They had a 2 hour rush charge that I was willing to pay so I could take them with me. When I picked them up at 11 AM the owner's wife said, no rush charge, you're a good customer. I never forgot that and they got all my cleaners business as long as I lived in the area. And whenever a friend or relative needed dry cleaning or laundry, guess where I sent them. That little extra caring and service paid off much more than the rush charge would have been.

2

MADE IN AMERICA

With all the products being manufactured or assembled outside the United States it's hard to say *Made in America* and still be competitive and profitable. If there were ever two competitive products and one was made overseas and the other was made in the U.S., the U.S. made one should be more popular if prices were similar. But because of our higher working standards, workers wages and humanitarian concerns, the cost is usually higher. People are very patriotic and want to buy American made products but many times the low prices outweigh the patriotism. It's a shame but that's how it is, especially when consumers are on a tight budget.

But if there is some way to honestly claim that some or all of your products are *Made in America* you should consider it. Can some parts be made elsewhere and shipped to your location for assembly? Or have the parts made in the U.S. and shipped overseas where it can be assembled by lower wage workers. Either way some of your product is made or constructed in America by American workers. You will show support for the American worker and let the purchaser know that the profits will stay in the United States. An appeal to the patriotic feelings of the buyer may be enough to sway their decision even if there's a 5% to 10% price difference. How can they not want to show some support for their own country and its workers.

Another option is to have a premium brand that is only *Made in America*. Your high volume products can be manufactured and assembled wherever there is the most advantageous cost and sold to all the low price buyers. But everyone doesn't shop *only* for the rock bottom price and many can afford a better model of what they are buying. You can see that in cars and clothes for the person who wants something better or the best. Create a higher perceived value by using the *Made in America* label and add some enhanced features. You will entice the more discriminating buyers who may also feel they are doing their part for their country.

The *Made in America* tag can be a powerful selling tool and should be used whenever possible. Use it on flyers, advertisements, mailings and product labels. Always be honest and tell your buyers what part of the process was actually manufactured or assembled in the U.S. It can be used for promotions and stressed during national holidays. If your competitors aren't doing it you will have a good chance to pick up all the buyers who want to feel some patriotism when shopping for their needs. Proudly say *Made in America* and watch your sales grow.

3

IT'S HOMEMADE!

Not mass produced, not machine made, not factory made but *homemade.* Somehow the word *homemade* sounds so wholesome, fresh and made with care. It's like someone has personally prepared your product like it's done in your own home. They have used the best and freshest ingredients with care to only result in the finest product that can be made. A product that excels in quality over all others that aren't labeled *homemade.* A product with little or no additives, chemicals or preservatives that you wouldn't find in your own kitchen. The vision of an assembly line filling thousands of jars and boxes quickly doesn't even enter your mind. This stuff is *homemade* so it's got to be better, no question about it.

With all the large corporations owning and controlling most of our food supply today it's hard to find anything that's really *homemade* anymore. Almost everything you find on the shelves in the supermarket or in fast food restaurants is mass produced, flash frozen or has all kinds of chemicals in it. Even though the FDA says it's safe, a lot of us don't feel we should be putting too much of it in our bodies. But the big companies think they have no choice but to mass produce to be able to supply all the demand and distribution needs.

But because of the time it takes from production to packaging to distribution to sale to consumption it's needs chemicals and preservatives to keep it from spoiling or becoming stale. A spoiled, unsold, returned product is not profitable, it can't really be *homemade.*

Fast food restaurants don't all make their hamburgers from freshly ground beef; it's normally frozen and formed before it arrives at their kitchen. Chain deli style sub shops may slice their meat in the store but it's likely frozen when they get it from their distribution commissary. They make your sub or sandwich fresh in front of you with previously frozen meat or seafood. At least the vegetables they use are fresh, we hope. They rally can't supply hundreds or thousands of retail outlets with completely fresh and unfrozen food and keep the consistency they require. So you don't see may of them honestly advertising homemade; people would catch on and be disappointed. Negative word-of-mouth would spread quickly and they would lose face and some of their image with the public. There's an old saying that *"You can't fool Mother Nature,"* but you can't fool the buying public either.

Here's where the smaller, independent or gourmet businesses can jump in and grab the *"homemade conscious"* part of the market. When the word *homemade* is associated with a product, *and* the public believes it, price becomes secondary. One larger company called Whole Foods loves to use the *organic* word with their products and that's fine but most of their prices are sky high. I occasionally shop there and find that their food is healthy and good but their service is lacking. If you can produce and market good ole *homemade* products and use unfrozen deli meat in your stores, you will be found by customers. And if you can also provide the *old fashioned* service that people used to expect, you should have an advantage over competitors. Doesn't *homemade* remind you of mom in the kitchen cooking by the stove using her own *tried and true* recipe? You just know that it's going to be delicious and good for you, too. There aren't many other places that can compete with that.

4

TARGET A SPECIFIC ETHNIC GROUP

When you try to sell to everyone, A.K.A the mass market, your product may become a commodity. Then price becomes an issue. The big discounters aren't going to let you win on price. They don't have to. That's their market and they are going to control it whether you like it or not. You won't be noticed anyway. You can't afford the advertising and promotion dollars. But the big guys won't be buying much from small suppliers and manufacturers of specialty products. These products don't appeal to the mass merchandisers and they can't rely on a continual supply. They also can't control ordering systems and *just-in-time* delivery. This is not their way of doing business, sort of like putting orange juice in your gas tank. Their entire operation won't run as smoothly as it previously did.

This is where the smaller independent business person comes in and seizes the opportunity. Provide a group of products and services that are not being addressed by either the *big box* companies or other competitors. Be courageous and smart enough to go after the dollars of an ethnic group in or near your selling area. This group of the buying public is waiting for someone to come into their market and supply what they can't buy elsewhere. Word-of-mouth advertising will spread quickly and they will become loyal customers as long as they feel they are getting fair value for their money.

If you, the business owner, are not a member of the ethnic group you want to target, how will you achieve credibility? How will you know exactly what products this group wants to buy and what quality level? You may want to hire one or two people from the ethnic group to work with you when developing your product line. They will have the close contact you need to select the correct items and maybe even supply sources. After all, they are probably consumers in this market themselves. If you ever want to sell out in the future, the people on staff may be the first ones interested. They will know the business, the market and how your company works.

Once you've established a firm foothold in the ethnic market you are targeting, strong loyalty may be established. This will keep others from just jumping in and cutting prices. You don't have to be a new business to target an ethnic group. You can add it to your current company. When the competition, large & small, starts creeping into your market share, it is the time to make some aggressive changes. But you will also need sources of supply which are not exactly mainstream, so do some investigating first. You can do an Internet search and contact your group's foreign consulate for overseas producers. If you get specific ideas for products or recipes for food, you can contact local or regional manufactures for a private label supply. Once you have your ethnic group customers hooked on a private label product it will be difficult for competitors to entice them away even using low prices. The more exclusive you can be, the faster you will grow and build a loyal customer base.

To promote your new business to your target ethnic market, you need to be very specific in your advertising and promotion. It does little good to advertise in the general media and newspapers where your potential customers may only be 5% of the readership. You will need to find out what they are reading or watching and make your presence known there. If there are any associations or meeting groups, join them. You can attend meetings or events or send one of your people. Have colorful flyers made and maybe coupons to entice their first visit or call to you business. Keep asking your customers for ideas and what new products they'd like to see.

5

HIRE SUPERSTARS

We all want the best possible employees we can get for the money we're able to pay but do we all take the time necessary to select them? You must remember that the people on your staff who have direct contact with your customers represent your total company. They are what can *make you or break you,* as the saying goes. If they don't please your patrons and *wow* them, there's no reason for repeat business. And without customers that remember your business, you're just another jelly bean in the jar. Great employees on the front line and behind the scenes are the foundation of a growing, prosperous and successful business. Don't underestimate their power in your company.

Superstar employees will care about more than just their paycheck and want to become an important part of your winning team. They will want to develop into a key part of your business so let them and lower some of the restrictive fences. Give them the opportunity to make small decisions without getting approval first. This will build their confidence and they will want to do even more. No one likes a superior looking over their shoulder about every little thing and superstar employees will appreciate the extra space you give them. Let them know you trust them and count on their support to make the company successful. The more comfortable they feel in doing their job the more creative they will become. Show them that you believe in their honesty and reliability and it will be returned to you in all they do.

So, how do you know if you have a superstar employee on your staff? You may suspect that you have a potential candidate when you hire him, but you never know for sure until you see him in action. Some of the things that will tip you off to their superstar status are:

- A self starter every day

- Customers make favorable comments

- You see it in their smile

- They easily earn coworkers respect

- Eager to accept responsibility

- Eager to assist customers/clients

- Happy to work on problems

- No attendance or punctual matters

- Shows confidence and self assurance

- Never complains about duties or assignments

- Likes to stay busy all the time

- Offers suggestions to build your business

These are easy to recognize because you won't see many of these traits in your average employees. As the saying goes – "they will stick out like a sore thumb." They will make your job easier and your business shine in the face of competition. It's like a value – added service for your customers and clients.

The next big question is: how do you find these superstar

employees and add them to your staff? They are not
and if they are currently working at another compa..
ficult to get them to leave. I am always on the lookout .
my personal and business life and can tell when I'm talking to
one who is exceptional in their job. If the opportunity arises I w
give them a business card and tell them that if they are ever available to give me a call. Then keep a log of where you saw them and
when. You can also ask their first name if it's not on a business card
or name badge. These can be your best candidates because you have
seen them in action over a period of time. And they are not putting
on an act to impress you, just doing their regular job, but better
than others.

You can also find them from newspaper and online ads as
well as from agencies. But only about one in ten will qualify as superstar potential. You need to inquire into their goals and past accomplishments and watch how they answer these questions. You
should see if there is enthusiasm in their attitude and not a constant
flow of problems and excuses. Once you feel you may have a superstar candidate, check a few past references and even school personnel if it's recent. Don't delay too long in your final decision because
someone else may recognize them as a superstar and hire them first.
Always be on the lookout for superstar employees and keep them
challenged, motivated and happy.

6

RUSH TO MARKET

The one advantage a small or medium size business has over a large corporation is the ability to react quickly to change. Smaller firms can bring a new product to market in days rather than months or years it takes a big corporation. The big guys have to go through any number of meetings and approvals at several different management levels before anything gets out the door. No one wants to take responsibility for making a decision that may not result in a success. There are so many departments that have to be involved that it's a wonder that they ever get it done. Not to mention the money spent on every step of the way. It may take many millions of dollars spent just to get a $19.95 product in front of the buying public. And if it fails to recoup the expense of bringing it to the market, it's hard to point a finger at anyone responsible, there were so many of them.

But along comes a smaller company with a new idea or product for a target market. There may be only one person or small group with the power to approve it and proceed. As Harry Truman said, "The Buck Stops Here" is a little more definable in a small or medium size business. They can do a quick test, change as necessary, and test again in less than a month in most cases. The initial release can be to existing customers online or in established retail outlets. Survey your first buyers for their opinion and any suggestions they may have. Also inquire how they feel about the price level and value for the money. If you have a mailing list for your target market get them quick info and possibly a coupon or discount offer for their first purchase. In the time it took you to do all this, the large corporation is just finishing their first meeting.

Where do you find new innovative products and ideas that you can rush to market? They are out there everywhere if you keep looking. Many are found at industry trade shows at a manufacturer's booth looking for people to bring them into a target market. Others can be found by searching the internet using keywords that apply to your specific industry. Some will find you and offer a ground floor opportunity. Be sure that anything you decide to pursue has a patent or at least one pending (secure for a year). You don't want to start marketing something that any competitor can copy and maybe under price you on. Also ask your current suppliers if they are going to be releasing anything new or do they know of someone who is. The more you stay aware of your industry, the better chance you'll have to be first to know what's happening.

You can also develop new ideas and products in-house or by using consultants you have under contract. If you outsource design or a prototype be sure to get a signed confidentiality agreement before revealing any specific details on the project. When you are getting close to a final product, be sure to file for a patent through an attorney or even do it yourself online at **www.uspto.gov**. Read the FAQ section under PATENTS for some general information. Once you're ready to produce the new hot idea, you can search for manufactures or do it in-house if you have the necessary equipment. Either way, keep it quiet until you are ready to reveal it to the world.

Usually the first one to market gets the biggest share of buyers once all those predatory competitors start coming in. If you are providing a fair value for the price you're charging, you can count on a big loyalty from the initial purchasers. So when the new idea becomes a reality, get it out with your name on it as fast as possible. You may just have your competitors frozen with their eyes bugging out and their mouths wide open! "How sweet it is!"

7

MAKE IT EASY TO PAY

Two of the hardest things about making a business successful are getting the prospect to find you and shop plus having them to decide to buy. Once you have accomplished those two things you're home free, right? Not really, because the final and maybe most important part of the process is getting them to transfer money from their hand to yours. If that's not done easily, professionally and fast, what's the purpose of everything else. Once you've done your advertising, direct mail, banner ads or telemarketing, finish the job and get paid. You have spent time and money selecting the products and service they wanted; now let them pay and be on their way. If you have pleased them so far don't let them change their positive feelings when it's check-out time.

Give your hard-earned customer as many options to pay you as you can. Different people like using different ways of paying for products or services. You can take credit and debit cards, checks (use a guarantee service for retail), check by phone, cash and even traveler's checks. An instance I remember was that all the cleaners in one general area didn't take credit cards or checks, *CASH ONLY*. By only taking cash they will need a way of depositing it on a regular basis and they are advertising to criminals where all the money is. Well, a new cleaner opened in the area with modern equipment and a little higher prices. But the smartest thing they did was to accept most major credit cards. They even put a big sign in the window about credit cards because they knew there was a big need for it in the area. Customers flocked to the new store and it became busier than all the others. Shortly after, a couple of the other cleaners added credit card processing and stopped losing customers. But they could have been the innovators instead of followers. The lost customers may never come back to them.

For *online businesses* the obvious necessity for accepting credit cards is a secure site or page. Any page that asks new buyers to give personal information to open an account should be secure. Make it quick and easy and don't ask so many questions that people give up and abandon their purchase. You don't really need to know their mother's dog's name do you? They can also order on the website then call with a credit card if they don't want to enter it online. Or let them print out their order and fax it with a credit card number. Another option is to mail it in with payment information if they have the time to wait for processing.

For *business to business* sales you can also use credit cards or checks. Many businesses still use checks but are making some purchases with cards that give them "miles." For larger amounts we have offered to pay for the overnight charges to send a check rather a credit card payment. Both are in your bank account the next day and the $22.00 overnight fee is less than the 2% to 3% merchant processing fee. And they also can't reverse the charge on a check should there be come disagreement.

Keeping ahead of competitors means offering ways of doing things that they aren't. Helping customers pay fast and easily is one of those ways. When products or services are equal and prices are close, easy payment methods may tip the scale in your favor. Once your customer base is happy with your payment processes, positive word-of-mouth will travel through your target market. They should all like the different choices of ways to pay. Make this part of every sale a priority and watch the numbers add up.

8

WORD-OF-MOUTH POWER

Positive word-of-mouth (W-O-M) about your business is more powerful than any advertising that you can buy. You can spend all your marketing dollars on full color ads, commercials, info-mercials and direct mail and it's still not as forceful as one person telling a friend or relative to consider your business. The person passing the good will on may have had a pleasant experience or feel they received a great deal and they want to let everyone else know, it's just human nature. And the people who got the W-O-M passed on to them know that it's sincere and was not from the company but from someone they trust. You just can't buy that kind of praise or referral because it's not sale, you have to earn it.

You may remember the old and current television ads info-mercials with Ron Popiel from Ronco demonstrating some new-fangled device that amazed everyone. When it came to the price that was reduced a couple of times in front of your eyes, the final lowest price came with a phase for W-O-M. They said that "if you promise to tell at least two friends, you can have it for $XXX.00." You may not have thought much of it, but some people really believed they had to tell two people, and did it. He sold millions of gadgets and I bet a big chunk of them came from people telling others and showing them the device in their homes. It's like a homemade infomercial that no one had to pay for, and with a personal endorsement.

To start word-of-mouth advertising you must do something special for your customers or provide a new and exciting product that's unexpected. Or solve a problem and complaint so convincingly and overwhelmingly that your customer just can't wait to tell everyone about it. In some cases they will even go out of their way to spread the good fortune that they received. If you go one step further than you expect your competitors to do, everyone involved will remember your business first. In today's market (especially retail) that over and above service or enhanced product is so hard to find that people pass the word when they get it. W-O-M is just a positive rumor that you always want to be associated with.

Another way to get W-O-M advertising and referrals is to have hotels and resorts recommend you. If your business would appeal to travelers, get to know the concierge and front desk people at nearby hotels. See if you can offer them a free sample, free lunch, free massage or whatever it takes for them to rave about your business. You know that when out-of-town people are looking for something that they will ask people who work where they are staying first. They will feel that local people will not steer them wrong and may have been a patron themselves. Keep these people informed of any changes or enhancements to your business and visit or mail them periodically so they don't forget you.

One age group that seems to be a great power of W-O-M is the teen market. I don't remember too much advertising for the iPod, do you? Once the first group got their hands on it and proclaimed it *"new and cool,"* the snowball started rolling down the hill. I'm sure Apple saved millions of advertising dollars by having its early purchasers pass the word. The same thing happened for those ugly but comfortable "CROC" shoes. They have since used the power of the name to come out with a clothing line. If your product appeals to young people and they accept it, an overnight success could be on the way.

You need to check on your W-O-M occasionally to see if it's really happening and how often. Asking customers if they are pleased and casually mentioning to send their friends and associates is one way. Another is to offer a gift or discount for anyone they refer who mentions their name. If they were pleased they might do it anyway but you're showing your appreciation for the effort they are making. You don't want any of your competitors outdoing you in this area. Recognize and use this powerful marketing tool.

9

FIND A BETTER WAY

How well do you know your customers and what they want? How well do you know your market and what's missing? How many times have you seen something new and said, "Why didn't I think of that?" It happens every day in some market somewhere. Just think back 20 years and you'll see all the things that have changed the world and how we do things. As of this writing, 20 years ago there was no universal Internet as we know it today (the web was something a spider made). Hard to believe, isn't it? How could we live without it now? Or a cell phone and iPod that everyone could afford? And what's a DVD player; don't you get your movies on those bulky 8 track tapes? I could be making myself look old here but this was reality, really. Twenty years from now even these new things may seem old fashioned.

To be a success and stay ahead of competitors, you don't have to come up with life changing ideas like these. Even small changes that improve current products, services and ways to deliver them can make a difference. You need to know what people want, what they are fed-up with and even ideas for things no one ever thought of before. Things as basic as how to make the ink in a pen last longer with no increase in price; how to let men shave every other day with no difference in appearance; how to wash clothes while you travel or ten minute dinners that taste like they took all day. And the Grand Daddy of them all…how to lose weight, painlessly. Did you ever notice how every new diet or weight loss program seems to create interest and followers? That's because we all, me included, can't seem to stick with one method and are hoping the newest one will be easier and more successful.

People want the latest and will pay for it if it's within their means. So why not find something they will want more than what they're using now and give it to them. Stop running a status quo business and become an innovative business. This doesn't mean abandoning everything your doing now and take a flyer on some idea. I'm saying that you should always be on the lookout for a new great idea in your industry and target market. Either develop it yourself or find it though a supplier. Or if you have the idea but can't or don't have the resources to get it to the market, approach a current supplier with the intention going in together. If it's something that could be stolen by a competitor, ask anyone to whom you explain it, to sign a confidentiality agreement first. Remember even small changers in current products can make a big difference sometimes.

One of my favorite shows is *The Big Idea* with Donny Deutsch on CNBC every weekday evening. He has many guests on that have new ideas and had many doors slammed in their face with NO, NO, NO! They explain why their idea is better and how it benefits the eventual user. They tell how they had the perseverance and persistence to keep perusing success in spite of adversity. I'm sure people laughed at the hula hoop years ago, but it sold millions. In fact, it's come back today with a new resurgence. An old product with a new twist (excuse the pun). Sometimes you have to be a little pretentious to get your point across. Don't give up on a new and better way just because a few people thought it wouldn't fly.

If you already have a business going and have this new product, upgrade or service ready to go, let your market know. Don't just put it on the shelf, in your catalog, or on your website, tell people in a big way. Let them know that you were first to the market and how it can benefit them. If it's going to make a big change in how they do something, back it up with a great guarantee. They may have to come out of their comfort zone to try it, so reassure them, and stand behind it. Keep looking for the next *better way* because your new one isn't going to last forever either. Someone is always looking for a better way to do almost everything, you can count on it.

10

GREAT HEADLINES

No this is not a Jay Leno bit, it's how your target market is attracted to your message. A headline makes your prospects read more and act on it. It may be the only thing they see when reading their mail, watching TV, or reading the newspaper or magazines. If you don't get them in the first few seconds they are gone and so is your message. They will never know your offer or information if they are not enticed to go further. Your headline's main purpose is to get your prospect to read or watch the body copy where the real information is. Get their attention and direct them to the rest of the proposition and the suggestion to purchase. Without it your entire proposal is useless and ignored.

Your headline should appeal to a specific market group, a.k.a. your target prospect. Clever slogans and jingles are neither, also cartoons and jokes can really do more harm than good. Don't try to be cute in a headline but be informative and suggestive. Remember you only want to make the reader or viewer go to the next step because they want to know more. Your headline should reach out and grab your target prospect, be believable and make him want to know more. Don't let him toss out the mail, turn the page or change channels until you have told the complete story and made your offer. The headline will draw them in and the rest of the copy will sell them.

When trying to create a great headline that will make prospects and buyers come to you instead of your competitors, keep it simple and direct. Appeal to something that you know your target market wants and will react to. If you can get them to do a double-take on your headline you may have them, for a few more minutes at least. Here are a few good ideas for headliners that may work:

- Parents Read This!

- Easy Weight Loss

- Your Car is Not Safe

- Attention, Restaurant Owners

- No Credit Check

- $3.99 Lunch

- Homeowners Beware!

- Stress Relief Breakthrough

- The Truth About Dentists

- Free Installation

- Sell Your House Fast

- Painless Dentistry

- Now Accepting Credit Cards

- Child Safe Toys at Last!

- No Down Payment

- Wanted: Clogged Drains

We all want to be persuaded to buy the best and latest products and services at the best price for the value received. With so many advertising messages thrown in our face all day, every day, we just can't read or listen to all of them. Try to use *Hot Button* words, but don't get so fantastic that it sounds ridiculous, just pique their interest and get them to go to the next step. Keep it short and simple and to the point. Great headlines will make your marketing dollars work harder for you. Use them on ads, catalogs, sales letters, flyers and your website.

11

UNIQUE PACKAGING

If you're selling retail to consumers or business people, you need to stand out and be seen before you can be purchased. Without something special, the large corporation's products will overshadow you and maybe even hide you from view. Unless the purchaser has come in to specifically buy your product, it may get passed by. And even if they did come to buy yours they may see something near it that attracts their interest more and may even reconsider their original decision — all because of how it looks and what the packaging tells them. Packaging can and does influence buying decision, otherwise everything would be in a plain brown or gray wrapper. Remember that big company products usually get priority shelf and display space. You have to work even harder to be noticed.

To attract consumers you may want to use some type of unusual or outrageous shape along with bright and bold colors. You will want it to sort of jump-out and grab them so they can consider taking it home with them. For business customers you'll want it to look professional and easy to setup and start to use. Business people want to spend their time *doing business* not assembling things and reading instructions. If it's something electrical, you can have a package that lets the cord hang out so the potential purchaser can test it first. Think of how you would feel if you got back to your office or home and it didn't work.

For food products and anything perishable, you will want a package that's easily re-sealable and can be re-sealed many times, if necessary. Make the part that closes the package simple to use so the customer doesn't need a college degree to handle it properly. Also what about a break-away portion so the entire package doesn't have to be opened unless it's all being used at the same time. This idea is great for frozen products so they don't have to be defrosted all at once. These little ideas can entice a customer to try your product and be a repeat buyer.

Other packaging ideas are to make yours biodegradable for ecology-minded people. Attractive, playful designs for kids' products that are safe for the under-teen age group. Show someone actually using or eating your product so that buyers can put themselves in the picture. If possible have different styles and colors of packages for the different seasons of the year. Show any guarantee boldly on the outside of the package. Bundle with related products and price it lower than buying them separately. Or attach a free item that comes with the purchase — any idea that sets you apart from your competitors' products and makes the potential buyer take notice.

Once you have an idea or two for *unique packaging* you can take it to a firm that specializes in package design. It's always wise to check quotes of several different companies and make sure it fits in your budget. They can fine tune your idea and make it shelf friendly so it takes up less space and more items can be available for purchase. They can also design in a handle to make it easier to carry larger items for home or office. If they have trouble getting it to the checkout area, they may just decide to pick up something else. A good packaging company can also come up with ideas for you and offer several selections.

Don't overlook putting a good chunk of your marketing dollars into creating and designing great unique packaging. It's money well spent and can make an everyday item into something special. It can make an undecided purchaser choose yours over a competitor's.

12

FLAUNT YOUR BRAND

Your brand can be your logo, product name, company name or your own name if you have a legal or medical office. This is what you want people to remember you by and tell all their friends. It's the first thing that should come into their mind when anyone thinks of your industry, product or service. You don't want someone to say they know a great dentist or furnace guy but can't think of their name now. You want your brand on the tip of their tongue at all times when they think of that product or service (or when someone else asks them). Brands can be very strong and the big companies spend many millions promoting them. How many people have never heard of Tide® detergent? You can do the same with a smaller budget and some creativity. It's an important part of your marketing and a way to stay ahead of your competitors.

If you have a retail business you can flaunt your brand in front of customers every time they enter or even pass by. Use attractive signs and window displays to catch people's glance even if they're not coming in that day. When inside your store or professional office they should see employees with logo wear (always clean) and your brand on displays everywhere. Even if you're selling another company's products, your brand should be right there alongside. How impressive is a display that says, *ROLEX at Crown Jewelers*. And by the way, ROLEX didn't become an overnight brand either. They had to work at it over a period of time. But when you think of a luxury timepiece, what brand comes to mind first? Even if you don't register your brand (takes time and money) you can use the little *TM* after it to show you are considering it trademarked.

You can also have give-aways and T-shirts for your customers to wear and advertise your brand wherever they go. And if you sell clothing items with your brand on it, don't overprice them; it's better to sell near cost just to get as many out there as possible. Useful items such as letter openers, small totes and even pens can help boost brand exposure. If your brand or logo can be portrayed by a dress-up character that can roam your business floor or parking lot, it all adds to the exposure. When you don't see your customers face-to-face, I've heard companies answer their phone with, "Have a great day with (brand), how can I help you." And don't forget to use your logo and brand name on all your ads, signs, literature, letterheads, envelopes and especially service vehicles. Which reminds me; all service vehicles and trucks should be kept **CLEAN** all the time. It's worth the time and soap to portray that image.

If you're planning to do any type of charity work or make donations to a worthwhile cause, always do it in your business or brand name. What do you think most people will remember; $100.00 donation from Donald R. Smith or *Donny's Donuts?* I rest my case because you can certainly see the difference. Don't be too humble when it comes to your brand exposure — be *in-their-face* whenever possible. And if your current brand is not very exciting, change it, no one says you're stuck with it forever. Do what's necessary to stand out from competitors and have customers remember your brand.

13

KISS THEIR BUTTS SERVICE

This can be so rare in business today that most of us forget what it really is. The old *take the money and run* attitude seems to have crept into doing business everywhere. From the grocery store and gas station to the insurance agent, who *WOW's* you with their service anymore? Who does business the way *you* want to and not how they decided you will buy. Some of us remember when there was a service attendant at every gas station who filled your tank, checked your oil and cleaned your windshield all for just the price of gas. The gas might have been two cents more a gallon to cover the service but no one cared. You just loved the extra attention. Why did that disappear in today's way of doing business and how can you bring some of it back? Wouldn't you stand out among your competitors if you did?

People love great service when they are ready to buy and when they have problems. If a business treats you with indifference when you are purchasing, it may be a real nightmare if something doesn't work out later. Whether it's a restaurant, hair salon, car service or office machine dealer everything has potential for some problem to arise during or after the sale.

I remember hearing about some type of consumer electronics store that had signs all over saying, *Problems 'R Us, We're Here To Help. Kiss their butts service* is doing that unexpected little extra with a smile, not a frown. You must explain this and train your employees to give it all day, every day. Their jobs really depend on it.

When people get that unanticipated helping hand and big smile while doing business, they can't wait to tell their friends, relatives and associates. It's just a natural thing to share what they feel is good decision on their part to buy from you. Let them be disappointed with your competitors attitude, not yours. After all, service is really the *attitude* you have when doing business or making a sale. You may get their money once, but may never see them again especially if they have other choices. Make those other choices disappear from their mind because they would never consider them. When it comes to outstanding service, *do it 'till it hurts* because the extra sales and repeat business will make everyone feel better later.

Exceptional and conspicuous service doesn't have to really cost you much, if anything. You may have experienced it in some finer restaurants when the owner or top manager visits your table and sees how you are doing. Not just some part-time supervisor going through the motions, someone who really cares. Also, when a dentist or his top assistant calls you the next day to see how you're doing, *AND* gets you back in immediately if you have a problem. And the owner or executive of a business to business calls or sends a handwritten note to thank a new customer for their business. Or the new car salesman that gives you his personal cell phone number and tells you to contact him/her if the service department isn't treating you well. And the sales person (in-store or on-phone) who refers you to another business because they don't have what you need. Leave them with their mouth wide open with surprise because of how you have really helped them. If you want that oh-so-valuable word-of-mouth advertising, it all starts here. Take the time to look at your business right now and see where you find ways to incorporate *kiss their butts service.*

14

MAIL TO CONSUMERS

If your type of company sells mostly to consumers rather than business customers, direct mail can be cost effective method of marketing. But, consumer direct mail is really different from business direct mail because when we get home, we take off our business *"face"* and think of other things. We want to have fun, enjoy life and spend our personal money wisely. The amount of advertising mail you get at home depends on many things like the number of magazines you subscribe to, how many credit cards you have or what you've responded to in the past. Why do people open some and toss out others unopened? Something catches their eye or creates a desire to know more about what's inside.

You must decide how much you want to spend on copy and printing but even low budget targeted mailings can be creative and pull response. Most items in consumer mail are lower priced if the mailer is looking for an immediate sale. Be more ingenious and original than your competitors and reap the direct mail profits. It's the quality of the mailing rather than the quantity that equals success.

Here are a few ideas for profitable consumer direct mail:

- Self-contained or fold-open mailers that are colorful can be sent "bulk" or "standard" mail for a lower postage cost.

- Use a current list, people move often and consumer lists become outdated quickly. Buy a current list within 30 days of each mailing for best results.

- Don't use only black & white colors unless you're selling Dalmatians. Even a third color will make your piece stand out.

- Show a picture of your product in the copy on each page.

- If a service – show someone doing the service, with a smile on their face.

- Make a special offer – be creative and different.

- Give several ways to buy – phone, in person, online, fax or email.

- Offer a free gift if they buy *NOW* and use a credit card.

- If using a mailing house, the total cost after sorting should be no more than if you sent it yourself. Compare prices and find out how long it will take them to *get it out the door.*

- If using different lists, code your responses so you know where they came from. Some lists will pull better than others and you'll want to use that list again.

- Lists should be submitted to your mailing house on disk, CD or email so they can be easily sorted for lowest postage. Ask them for their preferred method.

- Mailings of less than 500 pieces should be done yourself, in-house. There will be little or no savings outsourcing it.

- Have a follow-up mailing and send to all who have become customers. After their satisfied purchase, they are likely to buy again soon.

- When people buy something, they like to receive it quickly. Free delivery is a big selling point, offer it if you can.

- Have a deadline when the special offer will end and make it easily seen.

Make your products and offers *now items*. Don't try to sell winter coats in August or beach balls in January like the stores do. Direct mail is a right now, today, pick up the phone and order proposition.

Small businesses need to use direct mail dollars wisely to get the most *orders* for the *bucks* spent. Make your copy more consumer friendly and leave out the heavy technical jargon. Be creative, unique and urgent for the best results. When it works for you, it can be a great inexpensive way to build your business. Since consumers are always buying, why shouldn't it be your products instead of *your* competitors!

15

DO CHAMBER NETWORKING

Chamber of Commerce meetings are where people meet people with business in mind. Maybe your competitors are too busy to join or attend meetings and you can be there with no adversaries present. Maybe they even think it's a waste of time and won't help their business. But you can be there to listen and contribute. And you never know when you'll find the *golden goose* at a chamber meeting or event. Most of the networking is done during the cocktail or social hour so make sure you're there in the beginning. And if there's a meal, sit at a table where you don't know many people so that you can meet the new ones before the formal meeting begins.

Here are some ideas to make the most of your networking time at a chamber meeting:

- Arrive early enough to use the entire networking time.

- Stop in the rest room when you arrive and check your appearance.

- Walk around the area with a smile and assess who is there, and who you want to meet.

- Eat conservatively; it's hard to talk with your mouth full.

- Keep drinks to a minimum – you're there to network and meet people, not party.

- *Briefly* say hello to anyone you know—but you're there to meet new people, so move around.

- Have a short introduction ready to introduce yourself.

- Have a confident attitude but *not cocky*.

- Exchange or hand out business cards with all people who can benefit you directly or indirectly.

- Have a pen to jot notes on the back of business cards for future reference.

- It's best not to conduct business while networking—set a future appointment and call to confirm.

- Keep an open ear and mind for things you may be interested in talking about.

- Talk to as many people as you can without cutting anyone short.

- If you don't find enough people who can benefit you, make friends with others who may send referrals.

- If there is really someone special that you meet, set a golf game and you'll have 5 hours with them.

- Don't leave immediately when the function is over, meet the speakers and other meeting VIPs.

- The next day, send an *it was nice to meet you* note to everyone you have a business card from.

- Follow-up with all the people you said you would call.

Driving back from the meeting, you need to decide if this is the type of function that you want to attend regularly. If not, look in your local paper for a list of other meetings, there should be many of them. Most newspapers publish the list once a week, usually on Monday. Another source of meetings is a business journal in your city or a city nearby. If you have the time to attend and network, you should see results. You are representing your company in an environment where business people meet to benefit each other.

16

RALLY THE TROOPS

If you want to stay ahead of competitors you have to be sure everyone on your staff is part of the same team. This means getting together regularly and discussing what is actually going on at the front lines and handling problems. You need to have regular meetings with *everyone* so they can find out what the rest of the company is doing and you can find out how they are doing. By letting everyone on the staff know what new developments are coming you are making them feel more important rather than just a number on a time clock.

Monthly meetings are the best for stores, offices or manufacturing businesses. Always schedule for an *off* time and *not* when customers need to be served or attended to. A Saturday morning or weekday morning before you're open for business is best. By having your meetings in the morning rather than the evening, employees are *fired* up for the day and can use many of the ideas right away, that day. Keep meetings to 2 hours or less and *pay them* for this time. After 2 hours, your personnel, especially the non-office ones, will get bored and lose interest. Paying them for the time they spend in the meeting should easily come back to you in better customer service, repeat business and more satisfied customers.

Always make an *agenda* and plan to divide the time you have among things you want to discuss. Some things to bring up during your meetings can be:

- New products and services

- Suggestions from employees

- Suggestions from customers

- Procedures (new and review old)

- Correct and solve problems

- Retirement goodbyes and thank yous

- New babies, weddings

- Birthdays during the month

- Formally introduce new employees

- Employee anniversaries with the company

- Employee rewards and bonuses

- Attend to grievances and complaints

- Discuss any customer complaints

- Ask for new employee referrals

- Planning for company events

- Discuss what competitors are doing

- Questions from employees

- Create enthusiasm and loyalty

- Get everyone involved in the company

- Let them know how the company is doing.

If you have multiple stores, offices or locations, bring everyone together at a centrally located place. If someone is coming more than 20 miles to the meeting, they should be given a few dollars for gas. Always end the meeting on an upbeat note, something positive they can take back to their job with them. The meetings should be a *must attend* event and anyone missing 3 in a year should seriously consider *moving on. It*'s a bad example for everyone else.

17

KNOW YOUR COMPETITORS

Whether you're a mature business, growing business or a new business, you will have competitors. That's what this book is all about. These are other businesses that want to outsell you and *take your customers.* They want to be as successful as you do and are after the same target customers. The secret to survival and growth is knowing as much or more about them as they know about you. Don't think that because you haven't heard anything from them that they're not keeping an eye on you, they are.

By knowing the answers to the following questions you might keep a step ahead.

1. *Exactly who are your competitors?* — If you're not sure, check the phone book or the web. Not knowing is not caring. Find out.

2. *Are they big, franchises, or small?* — This will tell you the financial resources they have available. If they are on the stock market, get their annual report.

3. *What are their strong points?* — Can you do it better or at

least the same? Are your strong points the same or different?

4. *Do they have niche products?* Are any of these products patented or can you offer a similar product? Are they copying any of your niche products?

5. *Are the owners on- site?* – If the owner is absentee, it will take them longer to respond to your changes. Managers usually can't make major decisions.

6. *What is their pricing strategy?* – Are they expensive, rock-bottom or middle priced? How do your prices compare to theirs?

7. *Are they opening new locations?* – You may be able to find this out by asking commercial realtors or brokers or just driving around.

8. *How many employees do they have?* – You can find this out by visiting their store asking people who work there or their customers. Are they full time, part time or temps?

9. *How do they pay their employees?* – High, medium or low; the quality of their work will be in proportion. Find a past employee and ask them.

10. *How are customers treated?* – Be a customer and find out or send a friend to browse. If they are rude or indifferent you can have an advantage.

11. *What are their weaknesses?* – Poor quality, rude service, small selection, late deliver---do it better. What do you hear from any of their past customers?

12. *Where are they?* – Near or far from you and if a store, are they easily accessible? What about parking? Are they on a main street or difficult to find?

13. *How do they market?* – Advertising, direct mail, signs, coupons or very little. Do you think they budget more for marketing than you do?

14. *What are their hours of operation?* – If longer than yours, can you change yours and be more customer-friendly? Be open when customers are ready to buy.

15. *How do they react to you?* – When you make changes, do they counter or do nothing and how quickly? Do they try to outdo you?

If you know the answers to most of these questions, you're a step ahead of most small business owners. Don't ignore the competition because they're *not* ignoring you. You can't stay a step ahead of them unless you know what they are doing. Plan your strategy with all the information available and be ready to change again quickly.

18

CREATE LOYALTY

We all want customer's loyalty but are you willing and do you know how to create it? Do you even make the effort? You must establish an overall environment and customer atmosphere about your business that sets you apart from all your competitors. You need to be customer friendly on every purchase every time. It can take many contacts and sales to create a trusted loyalty and only one bad incident to destroy it. That's why you and your staff have to be on game plan 100% of the time. You want all potential clients and customers to only think of your business when they need your type of products and services. Loyalty is not won or bought. It's earned the old-fashioned way. If your competitors aren't doing it, the door is wide open for you to move in. And if they are doing it, you have to work at it even harder.

Here are some ways you can create customer loyalty:

- Thank them for their business.

- Convenient business hours (for them, not you).

- Specialty product selections for target markets.

- Convenient reorder reminders (B to B customers).

- Faster check-out and payment

- High value perception.

- Exceptional front-line customer service.

- Friendly refunds and exchanges.

- Follow-up after the sale.

- Rush service at no extra charge.

- Use their name often and smile.

- Personal service and attention.

- Welcome special orders and changes.

- Faster order processing than competitors.

- Small perk for regular customers.

- Special interest group services and products.

- Have an outstanding guarantee (and back it up).

- Ask them for new product/service input.

- Have a rewards or pay-back program.

- Immediate problem solving (to their satisfaction).

- Alert your best customers to new product arrivals.

- An open door policy for questions.

- Go out of your way for customers and prospects.

You may have noticed that there is not mention of price in this list because price doesn't create loyalty. Actually price creates disloyalty because those who only purchase on price will go where ever it's the lowest. They may be loyal for one purchase only and you may or may not ever see them again. Forget trying to compete on price and develop other magnetisms that really create customer loyalty. Make your business a pleasurable, no-risk place to buy and customers will come back over and over. Loyalty versus advertising can't even be compared, loyalty wins every time.

19

DO A SEMINAR

If your customer base is local or within a 100 miles, why not share some of your knowledge with your customers and prospects. The advantages are fivefold:

First — It's another contact with your company.

Second — They can gain knowledge of the "What's New?" in your industry.

Third — They can see your company and staff in action.

Fourth — They meet more than just salespeople.

Fifth — It creates a comfort zone.

Bringing prospects and customers in to your business for a seminar is going that one extra step to create a bond for current and future purchases. It will make you stand out from others who are not doing it. In fact, some of your competitors may even show up and that's OK because it shows that it's working.

When offering a seminar of this type, there are several things that should make it successful and profitable in the long run. Here are some ideas:

- Make it *free – no cost* to attend.

- Keep the time limit under 2 hours or people will lose interest or try to leave early.

- Make it educational– not a sales pitch– they can always hear the sales pitch in their own office.

- Try to get speakers or trainers from other companies or outside sources and supplies to give variety.

- Send a formal invitation or at least a personalized letter three weeks in advance.

- Make follow-up calls to those who have not responded within a week of the event.

- Have an open door policy for others who hear about it and want to attend.

- Offer to pick up anyone who is coming over 25 miles — then send a stretch limo or fancy bus to pick up several at one time.

- Offer some type of refreshments but not an entire meal. If they eat too much they may fall asleep during the speakers.

- If it's going to be longer than 2 hours, have a break at 60% of the time.

- Make sure a restroom is nearby so attendees can go and come back easily.

- Select your attendees carefully. You're better off with fewer, but qualified people.

- Give them something when they leave — a sample, a small gift and, of course, extensive literature on your products or services.

- Try to set a follow-up date with each one — within a week if possible.

- Have a question and answer session at the end and encourage questions.

These Marketing Seminars will bring your business customers and prospects to a closer relationship. Education is a great selling tool and your attendees should be satisfied if they receive worthwhile information. They may feel some obligation to purchase where they felt they got the most valuable and informative ideas. Competitors may try to copy you later, but customers will remember who took the initiative and did it first.

20

LOWER PRICES

There may come a time when the market can no longer live with your prices. Competitors may be offering comparable products for much less. Sales are dwindling and you see potential customers looking at your products or calling for a quote, but sales and orders don't follow. If you can, ask them why they're not buying to see if they feel your price is too high or that they saw it for less elsewhere. Some people will be happy to tell you if you ask in a friendly manner. Price is not the best way to build a profitable business but sometimes conditions change and adjustments are needed. Be smart enough to watch for those changes so no business is lost due to price.

This is also the time to sell the advantages and benefits of your product or service — a better selection, guarantee, service or delivery than your competitors offer. However, some people will stress the lower price. Have you looked at your price on the products in question to see that you're up with the current trends? Some products get better and the price drops at the same time. Look at computers and televisions; you get much more for less than you did five years ago. Can you reduce any prices to pick up sales and market shares while still making a good profit without getting into a price war?

Here are some reasons why you may be able to lower prices:

1. Your supplier cost is less.

2. You're getting larger quantity discounts.

3. Your manufacturing costs are lower.

4. You're taking prompt payment discounts from suppliers.

5. Sales have increased – can accept lower profit per item.

6. To meet competitor's prices

7. To gain more of your market share.

8. To move excessive inventory.

9. You've downsized your staff.

10. You want to increase sales to sell the business.

11. Technology has forced prices lower.

12. To clear out soon-to-be obsolete products.

13. To use in an advertising campaign.

14. You products are becoming a commodity.

15. You're selling higher quantity orders.

By pricing your products or services too low, you'll force competitors to react. If they go lower than you, do you want to lower prices again? This can be financially dangerous because usually no one wins, and it can be even more harmful to your business growth. You don't want to be lured into prices so low that you don't make a profit. If competing against a large company with commodity products, you can follow their lead in pricing but sell a little higher if you have value-added service. Normally, large outlets have an impersonal sales staff or none at all. You can do the opposite.

Great customer service can add value to even the most basic commodity items. So when lowering prices, do go below your bottom line. You want your customers to feel that your price is fair compared to the value they have received. Let competitors go so low on price that that's the only thing they have to offer. If they do, they may not be your competitors much longer. There will be one less jelly bean in the jar.

21

EMPLOYEE TEAM PLAYERS

In sports, the coaches and managers always stress that the team as a unit is *more important* than any individual player. If the team wins, then all the players win *together*. Individual performance will be recognized only after the team wins together. After all, the stars on the team could not perform to their full potential if the backup players didn't support them and contribute to their ability to stand out. And all the star players know this and that they would be much less effective without the entire team's support. Teams score victories not individuals.

The same is true for your business; when the company wins, everyone wins. The victory over competitors should be shared and credit given to everyone on the company team. Team players (employees) should be told this and made to feel like their job, no matter how small, contributes to the company's progress. They need to feel that they are really important and you need their best effort to succeed; especially against competitors. When people feel that their individual job matters, it's easier for them to perform at their best. Getting their effort will really make you stand out in your market place.

Here are some ideas to generate the team spirit:

1. Clearly define each person's duties and goals — a well planned offensive succeeds more often.

2. Train employees in secondary positions as a backup when someone is off or if a position is vacant.

3. Encourage employees' suggestions, discuss them at meetings and reward the ones you use.

4. Let employees solve minor problems with customers without prior approval — then have them explain their solution to everyone else.

5. Have and *open-door* policy with managers and executives — employees should not feel apprehensive about discussing a problem at any time.

6. Create a feeling of trust and respect — it goes both ways and makes employees feel important and needed.

7. Follow through on promises and changes or your people will remember and disregard these in the future as worthless words.

8. Publicly recognize outstanding individual performance in front of other team member — it's contagious.

9. When good things happen, reward the team as a whole. It will bring them closer together for the next challenge.

10. Encourage team members to help each other with the focus on the overall goal.

11. When awarding bonuses, treat all levels of employees equally, they won together.

12. Start an after-work sports team so that employees can enjoy the team spirit away from the company.

13. When a promotion becomes available, let team members suggest a candidate — they work with them every day.

Employees who participate in a team effort are less likely to leave the company which saves you the expense of hiring and training. When you have a good team, you feel less anxiety about leaving for a vacation or business trip. The team should be able to handle most problems and circumstances that arise if they work together. Competitors who don't have a team spirit will be left behind by *your* championship team.

22

BE A SALES PROFESSIONAL

Anyone can be a salesperson. You see them everyday and everywhere, but it takes desire, perseverance and hard work to be a true professional. It's been said that a great sales pro doesn't really sell, they help people to buy. Most people in sales just get by, selling the minimum and earning the minimum. These are not the true professionals. But a select few are the top producers and top earners. Why, and what does it take? Why can two different sales people sell the same products or services in the same market and one sells five or ten times more? Being a true professional and rising above the ordinary is the answer. Constantly seeking a better way to achieve their goals and honing their skills.

Here are some of the qualities necessary to be a true sales professional:

- Desire – Has a burning need inside to succeed and be the absolute best they can be. Some people are born with it and others acquire it. The desire to win makes everything else easier because there is no second choice.

- Ethical – Being honest and truthful in today's world

~ 73 ~

helps build a long term reputation. Even one dishonest or unethical act can follow you through your career. There's an old saying that "it takes five more lies to cover up one lie."

- Optimistic – Always looking for the pot of gold at the end of the rainbow because they know it's there. Knowing that rejection is only part of the journey and must be endured to reach their destination. They start every day with a smile and great expectations.

- Empathetic – Understanding the prospect or customer's feelings and motives even if they don't agree with them. Able to find their needs, desires, and reasons they will buy.

- Prepared – Getting to know the prospect and company *before* the sales appointment. Doing research at the library or on the internet so they know the prospect's type of business and how they can use the product or service most effectively.

- Conscientious - Having a stick-to-it attitude and not easily distracted. They are not at the ballgame or playing golf when they should be making sales calls. Makes a plan and keeps working at it until desired results are achieved.

- Good Listener – Knowing that listening to a prospect or customer gives them an edge in making the sale. Doesn't interrupt and makes notes on critical points that will be helpful later. Has the mental toughness to keep *quiet* and learn from each situation.

- Focused – Sets goals and monitors the progress on the way to achieving those goals. Keeps their mind on the end result and does what's necessary to get there and makes adjustments as needed along the way.

- Energetic – Has a tireless energy to keep going when the *"going gets tough."* Doesn't quit because the next presentation could be the big sale they've been striving for. Keep themselves in good physical condition and mentally ready for the next challenge.

- Experienced – Has been in the sales profession long enough to fine tune their skills. Is not afraid of new challenges because they can draw on their past successes and failures.

- Tactful – Doesn't say things that can kill a sale and thinks before they speak. Can change directions during a sales presentation as needed, based on customer's responses. Has the common sense to know the right thing to say or do at the right time.

- Creative – Uses new ideas to benefit the overall sales procedure and shares those ideas with others. Has an open mind to new solutions to old problems and isn't afraid to try them. Can use their imagination to stimulate new ideas.

- Persuasive – Has the ability to turn objections into benefits without the prospect feeling pressure. Can convince the prospect that the sale will make their job or life better because of it. Keeps the sales interview going in the directions of a close at all times.

- Concerned – A *sincere* interest in providing a great service to the customer and follow-up to make sure it's done. Handling any problems with any order in a timely and caring manner to the satisfaction of the customer.

- Businesslike – Acting and dressing in a way that gives confidence to the prospect or customer. Practices good manners and efficiency in words and actions.

- Savvy – Can sell the value rather than the price. Is clever enough to understand the customer's objectives rather than their own. Knows whether they are meeting with the decision maker or just a messenger.

- Wise – Knows it's time to stop talking when the sale is

made. Doesn't talk themselves out of a sale by bringing up previously unmentioned features when the prospect has already decided to buy.

- Customer-Oriented – Has the ability to feel what the customer needs to see or feel so they can make the purchase without remorse. Uses all the resources of their company to satisfy the customer.

- Enthusiasm – Being excited about what they are selling, every day, so it's contagious to the prospect and others in their company. Starts every morning with a positive attitude and a smile.

- Persistence – Has the ability to keep going at full speed when the *rejections are high* and the *sales are low*. Doesn't give up in the face of opposition, setbacks or objections.

- Loyalty – Is faithful and devoted to their company and all its products and services. Is a believer that their sales will benefit the customer and is backed by and honest and truthful guarantee.

- Confidence – Knowing that they will be successful because they trust their abilities and their company. Feeling they have a chance to close every sale before they even start. They don't worry about making their quota, it's a *shoo-in!*

Do these qualities describe you or most of your sales force rather than competitors? Your company will stand out from the pack with sales pros on the front lines. Go over the list again and see which ones need reinforcement, strengthening and fine tuning. Don't just talk about it, *do it!*

23

GET POSITIVE PUBLICITY

Positive publicity can be the cheapest but not always the easiest exposure to the public you can get. You don't want to see your competitor's name in the public view more than yours, so don't let it happen. After all, where else can you get *free* mention of your company or your products and a third party giving you a plug? Some people call it PR (Public Relations) but whatever you prefer, it's just icing on your marketing cake. It's better than advertising because someone else is telling the story and it's not biased. Don't ever be too busy for the press and get as much positive publicity as you can.

- Check the editorial policies and needs of each media in the media directories at your library and adjust your press release accordingly.

- Direct your material to a specific editor by name (found in the media directory).

- Timing for certain holidays or slow days will increase your chances of being used because of less news.

- Know who reads, watches or listens to each media to be sure you're hitting the correct target market.

- Follow-up with a phone call or email if your press release pertains to an event on a specific date.

- Take print media plant tours or studio tours to meet and get to know editors and reporters and other personalities.

- Assume when talking to the media that you may be taped, so consider everything that you say is *on the record.*

- If you work with a certain media on a regular basis, get to know when their deadlines are.

- Have some information available that's not in your release to entice editors and reporters to contact you with questions.

- Always have a contact name and toll-free phone number or email address in bold print at the beginning and end of your document.

- Follow-up to see who's using your press release and when.

- Request a copy of the publication or air-time so you can be sure the information was used correctly.

- If your information and material concerns a national audience, send to wire services and news services. They can be found in media directories.

- Timing for a publication's editorial calendar can greatly increase your chance of being used. Ask for future editorial dates.

- Include some back-up information to support your claim to be an expert in the field of the release.

- Use one and one half or double spaced copy so the editors have room to make notes easily.

- Make sure you have interesting news copy and that it doesn't sound like an advertisement. Editors have a BIG wastebasket.

- If you are announcing a product, show how it's different and offer to send samples for media review.

- Offer your free appearance on radio or TV to be interviewed or take audience questions.

- If your press release relates to *breaking news*, send all materials FedEx or UPS overnight.

- Before going on a live show, try to spend a few minutes with your host to get a feel for their personality.

- If your host is acting or asking hostile questions, respond in a cool, professional manner. Don't let them rile you up, be professional at all times.

- Always demand a correction notice or retraction quickly for any print publicity that's inaccurate. Follow up to see that it's done.

- Just because the media hasn't used past releases, doesn't mean you shouldn't keep sending them.

24

BRAINSTORM WITH EVERYONE

Keeping your ears and eyes open will bring you ideas that you would not think of yourself. You see your business from one angle but others see it in a different way. If you want to stand out from competitors you'll have to grab ideas wherever you can get them. And other people including your employees, customers and suppliers may also know ways you can improve your business. When possible meet with these people, even if it's one-on-one, and find out what they are thinking. Information is valuable and keeps you going in the right direction. Find the time to listen and act on it regularly.

Brainstorm with Employees: There is no one else who is closer to your customers on a daily basis. They see and hear things when you're not there or when you are involved in other responsibilities. They see what's going on, if only in their corner of the business and have ideas to improve products, services and procedures. Meet with them often and draw those ideas out and reward the ones you use. Never be too busy to listen to a staff member's thoughts and observations. Keep an open door policy for ideas and encourage everyone to come to you with them. Don't embarrass anyone who suggests something offbeat or impossible to implement. Just tell them you'll review it and go on to the next person. You don't want others to feel apprehensive about speaking up and getting shot down too quickly. You can also have a suggestion box but the *IN box* on your desk is better. Create an atmosphere that inspires and motivates employees to participate. You may be surprised when something fantastic is submitted and really helps your business.

Brainstorm with Customers: What better source of finding out what customers want from your company than the customers themselves. Most of them will have ideas that will make their purchases more satisfying and create loyalty. They also know what products or services they want to see in the future that will keep them coming back. Get out in your store(s) and ask them directly. Don't just say, "Is everything OK," but tell them you're really interested in their opinions, good or bad. For business customers, call or email them personally and find out what they are thinking and what they want. You will have to initiate the inquiry because the majority of them will not. You can have an annual open house or conference with the express purpose of brainstorming for new ideas. This is an invaluable source of information you need to grow your company. Customers hold the key to your success and growth.

Brainstorm with Suppliers: Suppliers and venders probably know more about your business than you really want to believe, but it's true. But if they know about your business they also know about your competitor's business. So if you treat them more as partners than people you have to pay and order from you may be able to pick up some valuable information and ideas. Talk to them about what's new in your industry and tell them what your customers are asking for. They may have some products or services in the development stage that you can find out about in advance. Try to visit your major suppliers once or twice a year to just exchange ideas and industry trends. Also try to see them at any trade shows where they exhibit or attend. For future ideas, keep a written or computer file that alerts you when new ideas are coming to reality. You want to be sure you know what's happening before competitors. Then you will have more advance time to prepare how you will present them to your customers and prospects.

25

DON'T BREAK PROMISES

Webster's dictionary defines promise as *an agreement to do or not to do something*. Promises can be made in several different ways, verbal, on paper, with a handshake or by email. For a marriage you'll notice that they make us do it two ways, verbal *and* on paper. In business when a promise is made and kept, it will help build trust and loyalty. And a series of executed promises will keep you ahead of all those other competitors who break theirs. When you make a pledge or guarantee to a customer they expect you to keep it. It may take several fulfilled promises to get a client's trust but only one broken one to lose it.

It doesn't matter whether you intended to do it and forgot or just promised something to get a sale. Customers who have had this experience with your business will not forget it and lose faith in everything else you say or advertise. Why should they believe you? You've already demonstrated that you can't be trusted. About half of them will probably transfer their patronage to one of your competitors who can be trusted. This lost business will multiply if you keep breaking promises and frustrate customers. You should not even make a promise unless you are absolutely sure you can keep it. Even saying you will try to do something is close enough that customers may expect it. A disclaimer or escape clause may be legal but does nothing but destroy trust and loyalty.

How would you feel if a friend says that he will meet you at the Italian restaurant at 7PM and they're still not there at 7:30PM? Or the car dealer says your car will be ready at 3PM and the total cost is only $89.00. You show up at 3PM and find out it won't be ready until 6PM and now it's going to cost $265.00! You buy a health insurance policy that's supposed to cover everything and your first claim is rejected because of a pre-existing condition. Get the idea? Doesn't it make you want to run from the business as soon as you can? These types of situations happen everyday and businesses do suffer lost customers because of it. Enough lost customers and the entire company is in trouble — all because promises were made and not kept. It's a situation that should not have happened in the first place and could have easily been prevented.

Customers will look at the promises you make to them as a test of your integrity and honesty. Passing that test will reinforce their loyalty and put them more at ease in the future. They will be-gin to feel comfortable doing business with you and it will be very difficult for competitors to lure them away. But failing the test will result in just the opposite. They will wonder if they can ever believe anything you or your employees tell them. They will look at your products, services and your advertising and question whether you can be trusted. And don't think that you'll only lose one customer because of broken promises. The negative word-of-mouth travels much faster than the positive. By not doing what you say, you will also lose many of your prospects that hear that negative word-of-mouth. And if it happens often, your business will develop a reputa-tion that turns people away. Let your competitors break promises but go out of your way to make sure you keep yours.

26

BE READY TO SELL

If customers are not ready to buy your type of products or services now, all the advertising and promotion in the world isn't going to change their mind. But when the time comes that they have a need, desire or want for your type of products or services, are you the company they think of? Is your contact information *in-their-face* so they think of you first? Are you easy to find and eager for their business? Isn't that why you've been advertising and promoting for all year? When the customer is ready — *you be there and be ready.* If you're not, your competitors may be.

Here are some things to consider so you are ready to sell when your customers are ready to buy.

- *Business Cards* – is your card in every prospect's business card file? Do you give them out often and freely?

- *Phone Book Listing/Ad* – If applicable, are you easy to find in the phone book? Are all the numbers bold, correct and working?

- *Billboard/Road Signs* – Can your product or service or

location be seen by drivers? Do you keep it lit 24/7?

- *Phone Lines* - Do you have enough phone lines to handle multiple calls? Some people may not call back.

- *Location, Location, Location* – Is your retail store on a main street that most people pass every day? Or do you provide easy directions? Is there plenty of parking available?

- *Reorder Cards* – Do you send reorder cards to customers when they should need to order your products again?

- *Give Aways* – Do they have letter-openers, cups, pens, etc. on their desk with your phone number on them and magnets for retail stores?

- *Telemarketing* – Do you make brief calls regularly to remind buyers who you are and what you offer? Do you thank them for a previous purchase?

- *Website* — Is your site updated and where prospect and customers can get valuable information and FAQs?

- *Labels/Stickers* – Are these on your products with a phone number to call for supplies, service or repairs?

- *Target Ads* – Do you regularly advertise in newspapers, magazines, or trade journals where your buyers generally look? Do you have an online presence?

- *Moving Signs* – Do you have your logo, name and phone on all delivery trucks and vehicles? Do you keep them washed and clean?

- *Trade Shows* – Do you have exposure in trade shows where buyers look for ideas and vendors? Do you also attend other expos for new ideas?

- *Direct Mail* – Do you send new information and literature regularly? Do you let them know in advance of any sales? Do you update your lists periodically?

- *Hours of Operation* – Is your business open when the prospect/customer is available? Not only when you feel like working?

If you're not available, open and easily accessible when the buyer is ready to purchase, they may just spend their money with your competitor. This should not happen if you are ready when your customers want to buy. And if your rivals aren't also doing these things, you may be the one to capture those new customers.

27

BUY RIGHT

In every industry there is a certain comfort zone where customers feel that prices should fall within. Be a little higher and they will expect added benefits to justify the extra money they will have to spend. Be a little lower and they will consider it a discount or *bare bones* product or service. A majority of sales will fall in the middle to lower middle price range because people want a quality product or service at a fair price. So if you want to make relatively easy sales and get repeat business you should have your price somewhere in the middle range. Only the real bottom price shoppers will keep comparing prices until they find the lowest possible. Most people don't have time for this and will buy at what they think is a fair competitive price. If you have been in your industry for awhile, you know what this price range is.

So if you are limited to selling your products and services in a pre-determined range without going rock bottom or sky high, how can you make more money or profit on a sale? If you can't really change the price of the goods going out the front door, then look at the cost of the goods coming in the back door. You want to widen the gap between the cost and sell price which is your profit before expenses. And that profit is why we all go to work every day and open our businesses. We need to look at how we can get our cost lower and still keep the same quality level our customers expect. You can only hope that your competitors are ignoring this and that they use the traditional sources. Traditional is nice for museums and furniture but not for building a profitable business.

Maybe you need to think a little *outside the box* and find new or alternate sources of supply that will work with you on price and quality. I always remember a long time friend of mine telling me; "Sell to the customer at the price they want to pay, then go find a manufacturer where you can buy lower." This very successful business owner is Roger Aurelio, Sr., president/CEO of New Supplies Co., a construction supplies business in Romeoville, Illinois. He has always been able to survive and grow during the 30+ years he's been in business. He has seen many economic ups and downs during that time and adjusted accordingly. When the buyer's money was tight he went to suppliers and made them also tighten their belts. He now purchases from manufacturers all over the world and makes a good profit while still offering his customers *better than competitor's* prices. He's very humble about his methods but I know he's a tough businessman.

Don't be satisfied with current sources of supply that have you locked into set costs. Like my mother told me when I was turned down for a prom date, "There are always more fish in the sea," you just have to find them. Don't limit yourself to regional or national sources, look around the world. Search the internet and write or call consulates in many countries to find origins of supply. They are out there and some of the best ones may not be doing much advertising or promotion so you have to dig a little to find them. You can also meet new suppliers at trade shows and expos for your industry. It's worthwhile to attend even if you find only one new supplier per show that can increase your profit range. And don't overlook all the directories in the reference section of your library. It's like a supermarket of sources. But one thing to remember is, once you have found a new and profitable supplier, *Never, Never, Never* give out their names and locations to anyone else. Just think of how much time and effort it took to find them.

28

USE MYSTERY SHOPPERS

Do you want to see how well you're doing against your competition? Or how well you're doing compared to your expectations? Many times during your day-to-day routine you may overlook what's really going on at the front line. People who shop at your store might not offer comments, complaints or suggestions because it's too much effort and they don't want to be labeled a trouble maker. Some will tell you if you ask but may be reluctant to point out any negatives. So how do you find out this valuable information that you need to improve your business?

To get the most objective information and opinions, you need someone who has no internal interest in your business—someone who will *tell it like it is,* good or bad, someone who doesn't care if you like the answers or comments because they have nothing to lose. Actually the negative information they can offer will help you much more than anything positive. The positive information will tell you what not to change and to reinforce it, if possible. The bottom line is that any information is helpful if you don't already know it, so get as much as you can, good or bad, but honest facts.

You have two choices of who you use to gather this information. You can hire a professional firm that specializes in mystery shopping and get a big stack of reports for an expensive fee. Most big corporations do this regularly (if they're smart) and analyze the data in complex computer programs. This is great if you can afford it and will probably tell you things that you never thought of. But, if you can't or don't want to pay the high fee, take approach two, find your own mystery shoppers. They can be friends or relatives who have no vested interest in your business, or people who are familiar with your industry or type of business. You may also find them through your Chamber of Commerce or other business organization. Be on the lookout for them all the time and don't hesitate to ask for their help when you find one. Pay them well because their work can really make a difference in your business.

Set up a list of things you want them to look for and leave space for other comments that aren't included on your list. A professional shopping firm will have their own agenda but should ask you what else you want to add. Once you've selected your person or persons don't set specific times and dates, let them investigate on their own and report back to you when finished. You will want to know the times of their visits afterward so you can do any employee follow-up if needed. Encourage them to be objective and give you the real facts. You're looking for things to improve not fluffy compléments. As I said earlier, you can't change things for the better if you don't know what's actually going on.

When you get mystery shoppers started at your stores, why stop there? Use the same people to shop your competitors. Sam Walton did this constantly, even to the point of being asked to leave. If you want to know what your competitors are doing, get someone in there to find out for you. Don't be surprised if you discover that they are also checking you out. When you get the reports and data for your stores and your competitors, lock yourself in a quiet room and compare. Look for areas to beat the competition and ways to fix any flaws in your own operation. Don't wait around with your head in the clouds, and a *high and mighty* attitude. There's always someone out there trying to take your customers. Don't make it easy for them. Have the information necessary to fix what needs fixing and leave alone what doesn't.

29

CONTESTS ARE FUN

Giving away a big prize will draw attention to your business and get people interested for at least the term of the contest. It can make a smaller company stand out and be seen in front of other big and small competitors. If you promote it and use it in advertising, new prospects may come to your door and you'll have a chance to capture them from your rivals. You will want any type of contest to be fun and interesting, even for the losers. You want people coming back to your business more often than they would normally for a chance to win something. Once you have them hooked, you will likely get more business than usual from them. And for those *not-yet* prospects, they will at least see what your company has to offer and may turn into patrons soon. Contests can make it more fun to shop with you than with competitors.

There are different methods you can use for your contests that will give some variety to it. The oldest and easiest is the random drawing. People will fill out an entry from and drop it in a big box or drum. Then usually someone who can't win the prizes will mix up the entries and draw out the winners one by one. The one thing to remember if you use this type of contest is that you now have names and addresses for a mailing list. You know that most of them have some interest in your type of business and would be good candidates to hear from you again. And after you enter the data into your computer list, don't just throw the entries in the trash can. Destroy them somehow. With all the identity theft going on you don't want to be responsible for leaving names and addresses unprotected.

Another popular way to give away prizes is to use scratch-off game cards. These come in all sizes and can even be used as a mailer postcard. You can have only one area to uncover with a prize noted under it or a loser, try again. Or you can have a game where you have to match things to win something. Even another way is to have your players collect cards until they get all of something to win (like collecting 5 different animals and you win prize A.) There is also a stock TIC-TAC-TOE game where you win with 3 connected Xs or Os. Keep it sort of simple though, so people of all ages and education can easily play and have fun.

Each contest should adhere to the FTC guidelines that say that a contest or game of chance should have:

- Randomness – No person or thing can affect the outcome.

- Prizes — All that you advertise should be awarded.

- Disclosure – Everyone who plays gets the complete contest rules.

- Non-Customers – Everyone who enters has an equal chance to win whether a purchase is made or not.

If you are having a direct mail contest that is also going outside your home state you have to be sure that it's not seen as a *lottery* by some states which have laws concerning them. A lottery usually has three elements which are *Chance, Prizes* and *Consideration.* If you eliminate one of these it's not a lottery and *consideration* is the easiest. This normally means that you have to buy something to enter and *must be present to win* may also be interpreted as a *consideration.*

You can also have a fun game where everyone wins a discount off a purchase or a free dessert with a dinner meal. Kids love to win anything, even of low value and it lets their parents see them happy because of your business. Make the prizes something that everyone would like to win or just something unusual. Let a fun contest draw attention to your company or store and it may just increase your sales.

30

TELEMARKETING WITH CLASS

When you're calling people for business reasons at home or in the office it should be done with respect and some class. Let your competitors be rude, pushy and unprofessional. The only way to have a chance of making a sale and acquiring a new customer is by treating people the way you would want to be treated. Hey, isn't that the old *Golden Rule?* Well, it's not so old-fashioned and it still works today and will in the future. Whether you're selling a product, service or fund raising your calls need to be pleasant, informative and yes, still persuasive. Anything else creates a negative image and irritates the person called who will probably just hang up. You don't want to make friends with prospects, you just want them to listen to you and trust you. If they don't get as far as your offer you have no chance of success.

So if you want to be successful when doing telemarketing, there are some things you should train yourself and your staff not to do. Write down a list of the ones that would pertain to your company and keep it in front of everyone who is doing your telemarketing.

- Don't talk so fast that your prospect can't get a word in, they may just hang up.

- Don't be rude or disrespectful to the gatekeeper or screen person, you may need their help.

- Don't use high pressure and hard sell tactics, they seldom work anyway.

- Don't be discourteous if they are not interested, thank them for their time.

- Don't disregard the laws in your calling area.

- Don't forget to reward your best callers who follow your rules.

- Don't use slang or off-color words during your presentation or anytime on the phone.

- Don't forget to stop selling when they say yes, you might talk them out of it.

- Don't deviate from your outline or script too much.

- Don't make promises that you can't keep.

- Don't speak too loud or too soft.

- Don't forget that the operator can be very helpful.

- Don't wait to send out requested information and literature — Do it TODAY.

- Don't forget to introduce yourself by name and company when the prospect answers.

- Don't call a restaurant during lunch or dinner hours.

- Don't forget to try calling your list by starting at the back for unprecedented results.

- Don't take it personally when someone hangs up on you, they don't even know you.

- Don't forget to say *Thank You* as you end the call.

Put a little class and respect into your telemarketing so that the person you're calling will listen to your offer. Many businesses need this phone contact to increase sales so think of the *Golden Rule* when calling.

31

PARTNER WITH SUPPLIERS

In times of economic uncertainty, two companies going in the same direction, helping each other have a much better chance of prospering. So why *go it alone* when you can have a partner who has the same general goals as you do, but is not a competitor. Who is this wonderful company that really wants to see you succeed? It's your supplier, of course. Did you forget? Their success depends on yours and many others like you. And if your competitors are not making a bond with them, you can and get those little extras, especially when times are tough.

Your suppliers can offer a tremendous amount of product information to make your selling job a lot easier. If you haven't taken a plant tour of several of your top suppliers, put it at the top of your *TO DO LIST*. If you're a big enough or a fast growing customer you may get them to share in your airfare if they are out of town. You can probably get great training in how to present their products for you and your staff. Remember, without your current supplier you don't have that certain product until you find another source.

~ Barry Thomsen

At a business forms company I owned several years ago, we had a different supplier come in once a month to make a presentation. We would always learn something new about their company or products that we didn't know before. It was a *must attend* event for all salespeople and customer service. We would usually have the meeting early in the morning so the salespeople could use the ideas the same day — right afterwards. Usually the representative would bring donuts or sweet rolls and we'd be one happy family all going in the same direction, with increased sales as the goals. That's how you can get the full effect of a supplier's knowledge.

Many of your suppliers will have color literature which will be available to you at a nominal cost or free. Never pass up the opportunity to use these product flyers. It's one more thing you can offer to customers to show that you're more informed in your industry. Ask if you can have your business name printed on some of them the next time they do a big run. Or you might be able to convince them to share some of the cost of your own flyers if you highlight some of their products. Either way, you're saving money on marketing literature.

One way to make a supplier need you and your business is to offer some loyalty. By giving more orders to the same suppliers they see a volume that starts to mean growth after awhile. After this continues for a reasonable time you may notice a few perks tossed you way — faster delivery, faster returned phone calls or email, a little extra in your order or maybe even pricing. Like anything else there will be an occasional problem, so don't make unreasonable demands and threaten the loss of your business. After you've built a relationship over a longer period of time you may be able to set up a volume discount based on a years worth of orders rather than just one. If you guarantee a certain volume over a year period, can you get better pricing based on the overall quantity? It never hurts to ask, but make sure you're *willing* and *able* to fulfill the agreement. You can also request a prompt payment discount if you're able to pay your invoices quickly. There's not much loyalty left in the business to business world, so when it's given, it's noticed.

Sure, you are their customer, but if they provide the products, pricing and delivery your business requires to grow, you need them also. Never take a good supplier for granted because they are motivated, like you, to increase sales. If they don't see some loyalty from you, they'll look elsewhere for regular customers and may just become tight partners with your competitors. I guess you could say that a good supplier is a like a good employee. Treat them well and they'll do a great job for you.

32

SIGN POWER

One of the oldest methods of advertising and marketing is the use of signs. Probably the first use of signs with logos was hundreds of years ago when a village craftsman put a picture of work being done on a sign. This was used to advertise to uneducated people or those speaking different languages. If you saw a picture of a man shoeing a horse, you knew it was for a blacksmith shop. Or a big mug of beer was a bar or a tavern and most people knew what the word *bank* meant. These signs were hung on posts outside the business entrance or in the main window to entice customers.

Not a lot has changed over the years because signs are used everywhere and by almost every business. Signs are a cost effective way to *advertise* and *locate* your business. You only have to pay once (and maybe maintenance) and they do their job for five years and longer. You can't get advertising in the newspaper, radio or yellow pages and only pay one time and it keeps appearing month after month. If done correctly this is a real marketing advantage. They should be attractive, informative and professional. If the name on the sign doesn't explain the type of business a short line under it should do that. For example, *Carol's Salon* and under the name; *hair styling, nails and massage.*

Always put up enough signs or banners so that they can be seen from all directions. Some local regulations will dictate where and how many you can use, but you may be able to figure out ways around some of the rules if you want to use more signage. One way is to have people carry signs during your busiest hours along the nearest road. There is also a newer company called *Ad Spinners* that have talented people spin around large arrow-type signs that attract a lot of attention. Another idea is to piggy-back a sign of a non-competitor which draws more attention to both signs. *Flashing signs* are banned by most cities and towns (unless you're in Las Vegas), but a bright neon one with different colors will get many people to notice.

If you're a home-based business your neighbors might object to a big neon sign on your roof, so where do you put it? On the side of your delivery vehicles or magnetic signs on your car which can be removed during non-business hours. A sign can also be used in a window or on the front door. And if you're doing trade shows or ex-pos, an attractive colorful sign can catch more attendees' eyes than the free plain one the promoter provides you with. Be creative so that you attract attention and passers-by.

Established sign companies can assist you in design and in getting any permits you will need. They can also advise you on the best value for your budget and provide maintenance when it's needed. A well placed sign will attract new customers and remind current customers it's time to visit you again. So if planned correctly, it can become a marketing bargain. Don't let competitors outdo you with signs. It is money well spent.

33

FORGET YOU – NO WAY!

Company name recognition or mental association with your logo is what can keep your customers coming back. Being, so to speak, *in their face* whenever they need your type of product or service can be like a magnet drawing them in. If they forget your company name, logo and image, you're just one of the pack again. If you're only one of the pack of companies that can supply their needs, you have to earn their business all over again, from scratch. And that can be costly and take time and effort, which are two things that you don't have much of.

Creating automatic repeat business these days takes more than just quality products and great service. It also takes recall recognition and remembering who you are. There are so many competitors out there flooding your customer with coupons, ads, deals, and sales offers, it may be too easy to forget you when it's time to buy again. And many of those competitors may have bigger budgets for advertising and promotions than you do so it's easy to get lost in the shuffle. But don't give up yet, I have some ideas.

An inexpensive or at least reasonably priced way to keep

your name and logo in front of customers and prospects is by using promotional items — little giveaways that may or may not have a useful value but are *free*. Most people like and appreciate anything that's *free*, especially kids. Whether they keep it or not depends on the value they put on it. And the value can be as simple as the convenience of finding your phone number. When you're in a hurry to order a pizza, do you call the one on the magnet on your refrigerator or drag out the phone book? In today's fast-paced world, convenience is considered an added value. Young professionals on-the-go would probably not be the target customer of take-home and bake pizza, they just don't have the time and interest to do it. But the mother who is a homemaker or works only part time will get a feeling that she is actually doing the cooking for the family.

The things you can use as promo items can be as simple as a pen or magnet or as upscale as a briefcase or article of clothing. It depends to some degree on your average sale amount and the frequency of purchases. If you're selling cars though, a free pen or balloon isn't going to do it. For these larger amounts, customers like things like a jacket with your logo or something for their home is more appropriate. You're not only creating loyalty, your logo is advertising to everyone who sees it. For higher priced models of anything, prestige of ownership is part of the deal. They will want their friends to know that they purchased your premium product.

If the cost and value of your promo item doesn't match the price of the product or service closely, it can cause other concerns. If you're selling ice cream cones and you give away marble desk sets, how does that relate? And if you're service is lawn maintenance and you give away leather handbags, your customers may wonder how much profit you're making from them. You don't want them to think you're giving them a valuable premium because you fell guilty about what you're charging them. Make it useful and appealing but not worth more than 2% of what they spent.

Things that are practical and somehow relate to your type of business are the best. Whether it's for everyday use, something to make their life easier or just the convenience of finding your phone number faster, keep it simple and relative. When kids are part of the buying influence, colorful fun items come into play. Kids usually like anything that's *free,* has moving parts or is shiny and bright. There are many suppliers of these products out there, so look in your local phone book or search the internet. Check with more than one to have a choice of many different products. The more unique you can be, the easier it will be to remember your company. And they can be located in any part of the country for your best sources. If you select your promo items wisely, you can create loyalty that brings you repeat business and new customers.

34

CUSTOMER FRIENDLY WEBSITE

Almost every business in the world today needs a presence on the internet. It gives prospects and customers a chance to see what your company is all about before making a contact via phone or e-mail. A simple design for smaller businesses or home- based companies will suffice, if only to show you're a real business and some of your products and services. In every medium to large city there will be many website designers just waiting for you to call them for assistance. Find one that's either independent or with a firm that's not too large. You can also buy software at your local electronics store and do-it-yourself if you're the type of person who enjoys doing it. And I'm sure there is a way to also buy a guide or software online so you don't even have to leave the house or office.

The one thing you want to remember when setting up your website is to make it easy for anyone to use. In most cases the people visiting it won't be computer experts and they won't stay long if they can't find things easily or navigate smoothly. Nobody wants to read instructions or take a class just to visit you. They will be gone quickly if they get confused or stuck trying to get around. Don't let your site slow them down or limit their options. Try to design it the way your grandmother could use it easily (unless she owns a software firm).

You'll need to decide if you want your website to just provide information and invite inquiries or to actually make a sale. You should have a customer service e-mail link that is answered within 24 hours but preferably much before that. Make all the pages easy to find. Have a way in and out so visitors don't have to exit the site and come back in to go to a different page. You can even have a comments section that people can tell you what is working or what they don't like on your site. Customer feedback is important if you want them to come back and tell their friends. It's best to include a *Contact Us* link on every page for convenience.

Keep your site fresh with new ideas and changes periodically to stop it from getting stale and uninteresting. You might want to have a *tip-of-the-month* pertaining to your industry or a general trivia question. People who answer the trivia question correctly can be entered into a drawing for a prize or one of your products. Keep a file of future ideas so that if you're very busy when it's time for a change, it's ready to go. But don't wait too long before you review your site for old information. There's nothing worse than visiting a site in February and seeing *Happy Holidays* still on the home page or announcing your special Memorial Day sale in October. If you can't keep track of what's on your site, designate a staff member to do it regularly and have another back-up person available. You just want to make visiting your site pleasant, informative and useful. And certainly not complicated and difficult to navigate to find things.

35

DON'T DESTROY LOYALTY

Just as I said in number 18 you can create loyalty, but you can also overturn it easily if you're not careful and don't pay attention. Don't make buying from you difficult, time consuming and an overall unpleasant experience. You'll drive your customers into the waiting open arms of your competitors. Think of repeat business as a goal you must always attain to stand out from competitors. One bad experience can make a customer stay away from your business for six months or more. Even if they enjoyed doing business with you before, they sometimes feel they need to withhold purchases to show their discontent.

Here are some loyalty *Don'ts* that can alienate customers:

- Poor/miserable customer service

- Out-of-stock items or unstocked shelves

- Owners ignore customers

- Customer service not reinforced

- Poorly displayed merchandise
- Leave them on HOLD and forget them
- Don't return phone calls or e-mails
- Have a sarcastic attitude
- Make them wait in long lines to pay
- Shoddy or poor quality products
- Have a no-refunds policy
- Business hours that suit only yourself
- Leaving a customer's question unanswered
- Have a long delivery time
- Employees ignore them when they're in the store
- Refuse special orders
- Drag out solving a problem
- Have a "NO EXCEPTIONS" policy
- Under staff your store or phone lines
- Opening late or closing early
- Reduce your guarantee to 24 hours
- Poorly dressed or groomed employees
- High price — low quality
- Make all sales final — no changes, no refunds
- Don't keep them informed on their order progress
- Cash or C.O.D. only, no credit cards
- Make the returns procedure unbearable

- Talking too low for them to easily hear

- Ignoring their requests and ideas

- Treating employees poorly in public

- Never say *Thank you* for their order

- Acting like the king of the castle

- Have a grouchy personality

- Have inflexible company policies

- You don't acknowledge a frequent customer

- Not training your employees effectively

- Closing before your posted hours

- Shutdown your business to go on vacation

Some of these may sound amusing but they are happening every day in some businesses. Your competitors would love to see you doing many of these things. If you could go back and look at some of the businesses that have closed, I'm sure you'll find a lot of these things being done. In tight economic times, customer loyalty plays a big part in your survival. Are any of these things happening in your business now?

36

PET FRIENDLY

Most of us love pets and many times we feel that they are part of the family. When we come home they are there waiting to greet us because they miss us when we are out and they have to stay home alone. We might all think that they have an easy life if they are in a domestic situation, but loneliness is their biggest enemy. While I don't believe that pets should be taken to many work locations, especially offices, maybe they can accompany the family other places. Older people who have lost a spouse and don't have many other family members nearby rely on pets for companionship and company. Since there is usually a strong bond between pets and family, how can you include that in your business and stand out from those unfriendly competitors? Your kindness toward customers' pets may even help your bottom line.

People like to travel with their pets rather than leave them with friends, relatives or in a kennel. But how can that be possible without leaving them in the car or van all night? A golfing friend of mine, Ed Williams, who owns the Heidelberg Motel and several others in Colorado Springs, has a unique *pet friendly* idea. He allows pet owners to have the pets stay in their motel rooms if they pay a little extra over the daily rate. This extra charge usually covers any additional time and effort it takes for housekeeping to clean the room and keep it fresh. In some cases he might just keep a few rooms separate, for pet owners only. He said that many travelers and travel agents know about it and make his motels a destination rather than a random stop. But he also has something outside to let passer-by travelers know that they are *pet friendly*. Every hotel or motel won't do this so he has his own niche market and has done very well with it.

I'm sure there are other businesses that can find a way to be *pet friendly* for customers who want to shop or visit with their four legged best friend along with them. But don't go overboard and just allow any type of pets. You don't want someone bringing a boa constrictor, a bee hive, or a horse into your business, unless of course you're a veterinarian. It's best to have a list of acceptable animals that you will allow in your business and post it outside and on your website. Don't let your pet lovers to offend any of your other customers, clients or prospects. There should be some way to keep them separated. The pet store chains all allow pets that behave in their stores now so there could be a way for other types of businesses to follow.

Being *pet friendly* can open doors to new customers and prospects who might not pay attention to you otherwise. If your competitors aren't doing it and won't consider it, you may stand out from the rest. You might even get to talk about it on a local radio station if you send them an e-mail or press release. Don't ignore the power that pets have with their owners.

37

YOUR RETAIL ATTITUDE

What's missing in retail today? I know it, you know it, we all know what it is: that personal service and feeling that your business is appreciated. Where it is? Why did it disappear in so many cases and how can we get it back? When your business has it, there is value added to every sale. That $0.10 extra for a tube of toothpaste doesn't really matter anymore. The good feeling the customer receives during the purchase is worth more than $0.10. It makes the shopping and spending your money experience more pleasant and keeps patrons returning again.

The big companies, some of your competitors, and the government offices have all but eliminated any personal service. Remember when you last renewed your driver's license? The people there are like machines and make you feel like you're just a number. Because, you have no other choice, you get the bare minimum of service. Don't they realize that it's your tax dollars that pay them? And the big companies bombard you with advertising and super low prices because they can't get your business with the sub-par service they provide. They spend millions of dollars to get you in their stores, treat you with indifference, then have to do it all over again.

The retail employees don't care because they aren't *taught to care.* How many cashiers in a large department store do you see trying to go faster because their line is long. Don't make me laugh, they probably get a little crabby because they have to keep working non-stop. If your competitors are not taking care of their employees, then the employees are not showing care to their customers.

So how can a small business avoid these pitfalls? You can make personal service with a smile part of your training and super-vision. A smile doesn't hurt that much, try it. You can only put friendly and helpful employees on the front lines for customer con-tact. You or a manager can monitor your employees in action and make adjustments as soon as they are necessary. Some employees will have a natural smile and ability to make customers feel good. Others will have to force a smile and be helpful only when it's easy and the customer is non-demanding. Weed out those less than natu-ral employees and assign them secondary back-up positions with less customer contact.

How much does it really cost to provide helpful and friendly service? Certainly a lot less than massive advertising costs or full page phone book ads. Reduce your yellow pages ad from a half page to a quarter page and use the savings to recruit and train out-standing retail employees. Your customers will remember the great service they receive more than big ads and low prices. Make your store so user friendly that customers won't pay attention to competi-tor's ads and commercials when they need your type of products. They'll only be at your doorstep. Let the big and impersonal compa-nies increase their expenses while you increase your profits. Make sure you and your staff have a super helpful and friendly attitude when working with customers and prospects. Put what's missing back in retail and profit!

38

ANNIVERSARY CELEBRATION

No, I don't mean with your spouse (do that privately). I mean with your business. It comes around every year and you might as well use it and get some recognition from it. Unless you opened your business on a national holiday (which isn't likely) no one else, including your competitors, will be using that day. It's your one special time to get some attention for your business, so don't pass it up. Include all your employees and customers in any type of celebration you plan.

Anniversaries can be used by retail as well as mail order and business to business companies. It can also make customers more comfortable because of your longevity in business. Remember, many companies don't make it past two years and some don't even survive the first year. By having some type of event, you're rewarding your loyal customers and picking up some new ones. You may even get some free publicity if you've been in business for a long time. So don't just assume it's just another day in business, use it to your advantage and let everyone join in.

The kind of celebration or event you have will depend on

your type of customer. What will your customers be attracted to: a special sale, a parking lot party, a contest, free gifts or entertainment? You can use a free offer for mail order customers like a big discount or 20% more if you order during our *anniversary week*. If you have large local business customers, you can have sales people deliver a box of candy, donuts or a specific usable item made just for your anniversary. People enjoy celebrating anything, especially if it doesn't cost them anything.

You could also use this occasion to announce a new product or service that your target market has been waiting for. Make pre-announcement statements in the paper or through direct mail to build anticipation. If your customers are all around the country, consider making a video or CD of your presentation and send it to them. Or do it by e-mail and direct them to a specific link on your website. You might want to have a special discount or prize for the first 10 or 100 buyers.

If you have a retail store, you can roll back prices on some popular products to the prices when the store was founded. Set up only certain hours for this and be ready to handle a crowd. It can all tie-in with a mini-party and free soda, food and kid games. A free raffle for an expensive item can be a temptation to pull in new customers. Have banners made for the occasion and if you don't put a date on them, you can use them again next year. Alert the media with a big YOU'RE INVITED invitation that you can mail or e-mail.

Start planning a few months in advance to give yourself time to come up with ideas and a way to use them. Ask others on your staff for their input and let them follow through on the ones you like. You're going to have your anniversary anyway, so you might as well use it to your advantage. You will probably pick up enough new business to offset any extra expense, plus some valuable exposure. Let your competitors be in awe while your business is getting all the attention.

39

SURPRISE CUSTOMERS

Did someone ever do something for you or give you a gift for no particular reason that was not expected? How did it perk you up and brighten your day? I think most of us like positive and pleasant surprises once in a while and we usually remember them long after they have occurred. When a business does something special or surprises you with a kind gesture, it's so unusual that it mentally puts them on top of your priority list. Catching people off-guard with a positive surprise can really build loyalty, at least for a short time. But 6 months or a year later the feeling of gratitude may have worn off and it needs to be repeated. Find a way to surprise customers, one that you know your competitors would never do.

One of my favorite places to stop in the morning on the way to the office is my local Starbucks. For some reason I seem to always go to the same one even though there are several in the area that I could stop at. I've also recently finished listening to the audio book, *The Starbucks Experience* and learned some interesting lessons. They have a never-pay-twice policy (my term, not theirs) so that if a customer drops or spills a product they are given another one at no charge. Even if it's more than half gone when it happens. Also one day a barista (Italian for bartender) decided to give a regular drive thru customer a *free* latte for no particular reason. The customer was so surprised that they gave her money to pay for the person in the car behind them. As the story goes, this went on for eleven cars in a row. One kind surprise gesture made all those people start their day with a smile. And don't think that they didn't spread the word when they arrived at where they were going. One surprise gift paid off eleven times.

There are many ways to surprise customers and clients so be creative and come up with some that fit your type of business. Things like a two-for-one offer that they didn't know about in advance. Or a free service attached to a purchase, like assembling a bookcase when it came in 40 pieces to a box. You might even occasionally offer free delivery of large items or on a large order. And a home builder or kitchen remodeler can give a bottle of champagne when their project is finished. It makes people feel special and may even take the bite out of writing that big payment check. The one thing that you want to see on a customer's face at the end of a transaction is a smile, but you have to put it there.

For some smaller customer surprises, give your better front line people the power to initiate them without prior approval. Let them know a general limit to what they can offer. You will also make your staff feel good doing it on their own. It just might be one of those win-win situations that everyone will remember.

40

CUSTOMER FRIENDLY HOURS

Over the years I've seen a lot of stores and businesses suffer sales losses due to inadequate hours of operation. When the business is open only the hours that the owner feels is convenient for them, not the customers, some patrons will go elsewhere. After all, they are the owner of the business, why shouldn't they set the rules? Well, you're certainly within your rights to do anything you want, but isn't the reason you're in business *to make money and grow?* You build a prosperous and profitable business by serving the customer, not yourself. People will go to one of your competitors if they have more friendly business hours.

If you can't or don't want to be open the hours necessary to accommodate your customers, it's time to sell the business and get into a different one. If a customer wants to buy a product at a certain time and you're not open, *they will find* someone else *who is open.* They may have been a past customer of yours and never knew about the competition, until you forced them to go elsewhere. Now your competitor is their current business source and there's a good chance they'll get all their future business too. All because you didn't cater to one of their needs, a need as simple as hours of operation.

Are you willing to take the chance of losing customers just to satisfy yourself? What's the purpose of doing this? The only result will be lost business and lost customers. If you want to leave everyday at 5 PM but the business needs to be open until 9 PM, you must find a reliable person or team to handle those extra hours. If customers want to buy during hours you can't or won't be there, you need to find a way to stay open. If there is any technical or product knowledge needed to serve customers, there must be a trained person available. Just having the door or phone lines open isn't enough. You should be able to handle any request at 8:45 PM that you do at noon. And if there may be questions that only you or your senior staff can answer, have a list of cell phone numbers available to reach one of you.

Your business hours are one of the things you need to consider even before you open or purchase a business. But most new owners ignore the time you need to be available for *all* your customers. Check competitors and be *open for business* at least as long as they are and longer if possible. If you're not there everyday at closing time, make sure your employees aren't shutting down five or ten minutes early just to help them get out on time. Many times, a customer will rush to be at your place of business right before you close. Don't have the door locked or the voice mail on even a minute before your advertised closing time. It's even best if you can still be available five or ten minutes longer. If that customer cared enough to reach you just before you close, you should care enough to be available to service them. You'll get a lot further ahead in the future if you keep them satisfied now rather than annoyed.

Make your hours *customer friendly*, not *owner friendly* and it will add to your bottom line. If you don't know what hours your customer want, ask them or make it part of a survey. Think of your average sale amount and multiply it out for a year. If you lost one or two sales a day, what would the lost revenue over a year be? Do the math and adjust your business hours to satisfy customers' needs. You will also satisfy one of your needs — increased sales.

41

TARGET A SPECIFIC AGE GROUP

Baby Boomers, Generation X, Generation Y, Generation ABC...who are these people and what do they mean to your business? How can one specific age group make or break your business and why? How can someone's age or generation group affect their buying habits? Why should you direct advertising and promotion to the age group that is most likely to buy your products? Doesn't everyone buy the same products the same way? Why should your retail establishment have a different décor for different generations? How should your advertising message be delivered differently to each age group? Why do you need to know all this stuff?

Whatever your age is today, 20 years ago you made your buying decisions differently than you do now. And 20 years from now you will also have another way of deciding how you buy products and services. Without changing with the times and generations a business can be left behind and wondering why. That might be why many of the large department stores are struggling when 20 to 30 years ago they were the place to shop. Trying to sell everything to everyone under one roof is not the way most shoppers want to buy anymore. Dealing with a sales clerk who is moved from one department to another and not being an expert in anything is not appealing. Today more specialty stores exist for people who want a bigger choice in a specific product area, plus the knowledge about it from a trained store clerk or representative.

By targeting a specific age group with your product or service you can zero in on more of their wants and needs. You can make the buying atmosphere more friendly and attractive to them so they will feel like they belong there and see others in their age group. Some of the larger companies have already done this, like Apple and the iPod, AARP with insurance and travel discounts, the Gap with trendy teen clothes, and Cool Cuts for kid's haircuts. If you go into a teen clothing store (I used to take my daughter) you will hear loud music and one wall is bound to have some flashy video on. I guess this makes them comfortable and they want to buy more. Not me though, I'll take the quiet background music with the professional sales person dressed in something other than jeans.

If you want to sell to more than one age group and have a retail store you can make separate areas with partitions for each group with different products and sales people who match and dress like the group they are selling to. Just don't let any loud music in one area be heard in another area. If you sell via commercials or direct mail, have different messages for each group and don't mention other groups in your messages. Keep everything geared to the age group you're focusing on. We all love our parents but don't really want to dress like them or listen to the same music. Make your business a place they want to visit more often than your competitors.

42

HIGH ROLLERS, MAYBE

High Rollers, meaning customers who buy a lot of your products or services, can be a plus or minus. Of course you want the sales, but at what cost? Most of your big customers will be happy with great products, service and competitive prices. But others will demand more and more and push you to your limits or into a corner. These are the ones that will make you decide if they're really worth it. Is the gain you receive worth the cost and aggravation that is needed to keep that customer? Don't get all worried that every *high roller* (in Vegas they call them Whales) is a troublesome case, but the few out there that are make you cautious about them all and with big dollars at stake you need to be cautious.

The first consideration is obvious — are they profitable? Do you make money from them, and can you serve them without additional expense? Most businesses offer some type of discount or reduced price for large quantity purchases, and this is fine. The larger sale allows you to purchase or manufacture at a lower cost and increases profits across the board. The bigger sales will also increase the value of your business, because the first thing a buyer looks at is total sales. But what, if anything, do you have to give up to get those sales? Normally a little recognition of their importance to your company and calling them by name will satisfy the average *high roller.* Remember, they need to make this large purchase somewhere, and if you make it easy, affordable and friendly to buy from you, why should they change? Just remember that your competitors are always looking for ways to steal them away.

These *high rollers* are usually very busy and their purchase or order from you is just one of many things on their *to-do list.* They may delegate some of the buying procedure but they are there in the background observing. So the easier you make it for them, the more likely they are to return. Even assigning a special person or account number can reduce any stress or confusion during repeat business. Your employees should know who these *high rollers* are and how to handle them correctly. Don't let a novice or trainee get involved and frustrate them, Have a plan or special procedure in place for them. Be sure everyone on your staff knows what to do or how to handle them.

The one thing you can't let happen is having a *high roller* tell you how to run your business. Suggestions are great, but demands are not. Offer a competitive price and V.I.P. service, but don't let *them tell you* what they are going to pay. Several big discount stores have tried to do this to smaller suppliers and backed them into a corner. If their demands put your company in trouble and after a while you can't meet the demands they'll probably walk away and go to your competitor. Don't ever put your company in this position — you may not survive. And don't beg for their business, just offer your best products, service and price, but you make the decisions, not them, on price.

Once you have a *high roller* on your customer list, a few perks and extras are OK. Birthday, anniversary and holiday gifts are always a nice touch. But don't make any gift or extra service look like you are buying their business — you just want to thank them for it. And never offer gifts before a sale is made, it looks like a bribe, and you don't want to give that impression. A personal acknowledgement or note from you, the owner, goes a long way in showing their business is appreciated. Most of them don't have time to read long letters anyway.

Profitable *high rollers* are always in demand, so don't take the good ones for granted. Your competitors are always out there trying to lure them away from you. Don't let a long time, regular *high roller* customer get lost in the shuffle; give them the recognition and service they deserve. They will keep you happy with increased sales and profits. And if you take them for granted, Mr. Competitor will have a big smile on his face.

43

LISTEN, LISTEN, LISTEN

I've heard an old adage that says "You can be more successful using your ears than your mouth." Maybe that's why we all have two ears and only one mouth. Listening is an art that some people are born with and others need to acquire. Either way, it's something you need to master if you are in business and meet or talk to customers and clients. While you are listening, you need to really hear what people are saying and be able to remember and use it to your advantage. You can pick up some valuable information and ideas from the people that you are listening to if you are paying attention. Let your competitors talk more than listen and you'll be a step ahead of them. As a business person, you should be listening to at least four different things; your customers, your employees, your suppliers and your own intuition and insight. Following are some reasons to pay close attention to each one.

Customers: These are the people that support your company, allow you to make a profit and provide the funds to pay your bills. If they are talking about your business, it's important that you hear and remember what they say and how they feel. Customers don't usually speak up unless there is something on their mind that they are concerned with. So be sure that you listen and address their concerns sincerely and promptly. Customers will also tell you what they would like to see you business change or offer to them in the future. This is a golden opportunity to find out what will help you grow and prosper. These are people who are saying that they will pay you if you listen and act on their requests. Don't tell them what they should buy, but listen to what *they want* to buy. Listening to what customers have to say can also save you thousands of market research dollars and put you more in touch with your target market.

Employees: The people who work for your business, your associates, know more about your company than you think they do. They also see things from a different perspective than you and your upper level managers. They may have ideas for new products or services, procedures, and ways of improving customer service. Many will have more direct or indirect contact with your customers than you do and hear valuable information that you need to grow your business. When they want to tell you what they know and have observed you should make the time to listen. Either have an open door policy or set specific times aside to listen to any and all of your employees. It makes them also feel important and a significant part of the team.

Suppliers: The companies and people who provide your business with the products you sell and other items to keep you operating, also see you from a different angle. They also know what's going on in other areas of your market and what some of your competitors are doing. Asking them what new products are on the way and listening to their response is very important to keep up with and stay ahead of competitors. Suppliers have the technical knowledge about your products and can assist with back-up sales support. They are also there to help solve after-sale problems that require expertise that you don't have. Also listen and heed their advice on any coming shortages or price increases. They have valuable information.

Your Intuition: After being in business for awhile you will have a little voice in your mind giving you ideas based on what's happening around you. Your insight and observation of the market and competitors will tell you what changes to make and which direction to go. Listen to your intuition because it's based on your ambition and desire to succeed. Many times your feelings about market changes and ideas can't be verified by the facts but you just feel that you are making the correct decisions. These decisions can give you a jump on competitors who may wait for more facts. Believe in yourself and act if intuition tells you it's right.

So listen and gather information before you speak or act on important decisions. Most people will respect a listener more than someone who talks more. Listening may be your winning success secret.

44

TRAIN, TRAIN, TRAIN

In most cases the owner of a business can't meet, service and process every customer or client they do business with so they hire employees to stand in for them. But are these employees doing the job you need them to do so that your company can prosper and grow? Employees can be only as good as you train them to be. And they will only stay as good with proper instruction, encouragement and supervision. When employee performance slides, it can take company growth and repeat sales with it. Companies have failed or dug a hole for themselves that's hard to get out of by the poor performance of its staff. Competitors will jump in and grab customers faster than you can blink your eyes. In many cases, it's only human nature to do the least acceptable job that you will allow. By tolerating below par job performance from even a few employees, it will become infectious throughout your company. If it's too much trouble for you, the owner, to care, why should they?

Initial training and the consistent reinforcement of that training is the key to top employee performance. When supervision is non existent or lacking, people will begin to do things the way *they* want to, not how they were trained to do them. Observing an

The Jelly Bean Principle ~

employee in the process of doing their job will quickly tell you whether a refresher class is necessary. You will know right away if they are performing the way you trained them and if more training is now needed. Remember that they are representing you and your company when they talk to customers and leave a lasting impression. They must be not only trained adequately but convinced that their performance really matters and is necessary for the growth of the entire business. Explain that if you build a house of cards and take away one at the bottom, the entire structure crumbles and you have to start over again.

So how much training is really necessary? How long should it take and who should do it? To be effective training should last as long as it takes to learn how to work with a customer professionally. Long enough for an employee to answer most of the questions a customer might bring up and feel comfortable doing it. And they must know all about the company's products and services. Long enough to know the products' benefits and advantages and which ones are best suited to each customer's needs. The customer looks to your people as experts in your industry and wants to rely on their help and advice. If the person they are working with is unsure of themselves or their answers, if reflects on the entire business. It's like telling the customer "try us at your own risk." How many of us really want to do that? Think of how one under trained employee makes the rest of the staff look. Does anyone really know what's going on here? Are your competitor's employees better trained than yours?

All your supervisors and managers must also be trained to watch what is going on, not just walking around giving orders and assignments. You have put them in their supervisory position to be your eyes and ears when you're not able to do it yourself. They should also be trained and reminded of the goals of the company and the procedures that have always helped it grow. Regular meetings with middle level managers and supervisors are necessary for owners and upper level people to receive the feedback that is needed to outdo competitors. Training is not a one time event but an ongoing process to fine tune employees into doing their very best and keeping your business a step ahead of competitors.

45

LEARN, LEARN, LEARN

Knowledge is power and the more you have and learn on a constant basis, the more ammunition you have to battle those pesky competitors out there. When you think you are too old or have been in business so long that you don't have to learn any more, it's time to put the *For Sale* sign out. Learning about the business atmosphere in general and changes in your industry is a continual journey that never ends. Being a professional business owner means that you are always learning, reading, studying, and perfecting your skills to grow and promote your business. Those that don't or lose interest are quickly moved aside so that competitors who do can pass them by. The business world doesn't stand still but is in constant motion to improve itself and everyone in it.

Some of the best places to learn more about your industry are at conventions and trade shows. Just walking the aisles at an expo can tell you a lot that you may not know was now happening in your industry. Attending a symposium or classes at an industry conference can bring you up to date on the latest developments and plant ideas to advance your business. Most of these are two hours or less and are time and money well spent. If you don't see your competitors in there with you then you'll walk out with an advantage.

Other sources of learning are local college courses and online universities to brush up on areas where you need reinforcement. You can also sign up for free classes at www.sba.gov about many different small business subjects. There are also many business seminars that travel to most of the big cities year-round and you may get a direct mail piece announcing them. If the subject matter in the brochure can help your business, travel to the nearest city to attend the seminar. There are several TV shows that feature success stories and ideas, such as *Business Nation, The Big Idea* and *Kitchen Nightmares* to name just a few. Learning doesn't always mean sitting in a classroom. It's real life observation, too.

I'm also a big advocate of learning from all different books and recorded tapes. I have bookcases full of all kinds of business books and books on tapes or CDs. They're in my office at work and at home. I just feel that a good business book (paper or audio) can give you ideas, suggestions and solutions to problems that you can't find anywhere else. When I listen to an audio book in the car, I know I will hear it again in a couple of months. You can't remember everything the first time or you may not need some of the information until the next time you hear it. In hard copy books, I'll sometimes mark pages with a paper clip if there is some unusual or important information. You may have a future situation where you need help quickly and refer back to the book with the answers.

I don't think you can have too many books, even if many are on the same business subject. Sometimes there are ideas in books that are 10 to 20 years old that will work just as well today. Every time I see a new book from a famous business person come out, I have to get it. If they are so successful, I want to know what they know that I don't. If I can get even one or two new ideas to try, I know that I've got my money's worth. Several books on the same business subject area will give you each author's perspective which may be different from the others. Then you can decide for yourself what will work best in your situation or use parts of all of them. *Never* throw a business book out. Find a place to keep it. You may need the information in it a year or longer from now. Most bookshelves are deep enough to store books two deep and I put the taller ones in the back. Books are like your kid's baby pictures; 10, 20 or 40 years from now, you'll still want to look at them.

So don't stop learning if you want to be a professional in your business field and rise above competitors. Keep those wheels in your mind turning and producing ideas by adding fuel to them regularity. And don't forget to share all that new knowledge with others as suggested in Principles #43 and #45. Being book smart *and* street smart has a way of making champions in business.

46

TEACH, TEACH, TEACH

Sharing your knowledge and skills will not only help those who are learning but enhance your own skills and dexterity. Teaching people business and life lessons will also make you appear to be an expert in your field or industry. When you're an expert, prospects and customers will look to your business as the place for the latest innovations as well as safety in purchasing. When your competitors are relaxing with their feet up on their desk, you can be out there spreading good will. People will usually remember the experts that taught them valuable information and they will be good candidates for customers in the near future. Be that expert and add value to your company.

Some of the best places to share your knowledge are at a local college, as a radio/TV guest, at internet classes and with your own employees. When teaching at a college or university you will probably be paid for the class you teach or are a quest speaker at. Don't ask for or expect too much, the experience and exposure can be worth more than money. To get the college to request and hire you for an assignment, send a proposal and resume to the head of the business school or department. Your business tenure may be more important than your past education so highlight all your accomplishments and successes. And be sure to mention any books and articles you have had published. Your objective is to teach real-life experiences in the business world not just textbook lessons. What you learned in the real world is rarely in textbooks.

You can also teach a part of your business knowledge at a Chamber of Commerce or Better Business Bureau meeting in your town or one nearby. They probably won't be able to pay you but you'll probably get a free lunch or dinner. If you entertain questions at the end, you'll find out what a lot of local business people are thinking. And don't overlook the education venue of the future, online classes. Phoenix University, Westwood College, DeVry University and others are going into it big time. You can probably find a subject area that is right for your field of expertise. Send to or e-mail several of them that offer business classes and see what they are looking for in instructors and offer your services. Now here's a teaching job you can do in your pajamas and slippers or from your office during lunch. Don't be too surprised if one of your competitors shows up in your class. If it happens, consider it a compliment.

Another good group to teach a class to is your suppliers and their reps. Set up a class at your location or rent a room at a local hotel or even a vacant room at a college. Teach them what it takes to sell their products and request more back-up resources. Then tell them what customers are requesting and what they should be doing research on first. If you're their customer and they want to grow they should listen to you. Turn yourself into an expert by teaching what you know best and move your competitors to second-best.

47

GIVE FRONT LINE AUTHORITY

In any sales environment, there will always be front line people who have direct contact with your customers. Hopefully you have selected your most cordial and knowledgeable employees for this important part of your business. In many cases, they will even get to know your customers better than you, the owner, does. Good front line people can supply customer satisfaction, create repeat business, referrals and loyalty. It doesn't matter whether it's a retail or business to business situation, they will get to know your customers. And your customers will get to know them, especially the *good ones* and the *bad ones*. While your big competitors insist that their front line people follow *the book* like robots, you can let your good people make minor decisions on their own.

Most sales of any product or service will go smoothly and your customer will be pleased with their purchase. But like life itself, occasionally something can go wrong and usually does. Isn't there a guy named *Murphy* who said this first? Maybe in our next life things will all go perfectly, but certainly not here. But it's not a question of whether something will go wrong, it's how well you handle it. And the most important factor in the resolution of a problem is how *quickly* you resolve it to the *customer's satisfaction.* Speed but not a rash decision, will be long remembered and can actually increase loyalty and repeat business. People are always very busy these days and want their purchase to run smoothly or to be fixed fast if it doesn't.

Look at it from your customer's perspective: they purchased something from you in good faith, paid for it and it's not right. Why should they wait to have you make it right any longer than is absolutely necessary? You didn't wait to take their order and money. Please remember that fixing an existing problem is just as important as or even more so than taking the next new order. As I've said before, think of the long term value of a customer, not just one sale. A disgruntled person whose problem wasn't solved quickly will spread negative word-of-mouth faster than you can sneeze.

One way to resolve some of these minor mishaps quickly is to give your front line people some authority to do it. They will usually be the first to hear about any problem and if they can solve it *on the spot,* your customer will be impressed — so impressed that they will probably give you positive word-of-mouth praise to everyone they know. You solved their problem much faster than they expected and turned a negative into a positive. Giving your front line people this authority, with a reasonable limit, is providing outstanding customer service that your competitors may not be doing. Your customers will eventually forget the problem but will remember how it was solved. And your employees will also feel a sense of accomplishment and good will.

One way to let front line employees solve these occasional situations quickly is to set a limit of how far they can go before getting further approval. I've heard about one company that set up a monthly fund of $XXXs that front line employees can use to solve problems quickly with customers. Once the fund is used up, if it actually is, a supervisor must give them final approval. When and if they ever get to that point, a supervisor will always be readily available to make a quick decision. Rarely does it get to that point but they are prepared if it does. Each month, the fund stats are at the full amount for the employees to use again. This way the owners can see what it's costing to solve problems and make any adjustments to eliminate reoccurring ones. The amount spent to solve problems on-the-spot is usually much less than the lifetime value of a customer. This is money well spent because it helps your front line employees save face and makes the customer leave with a smile. And when customers leave smiling, they come back.

48

GREAT TELEPHONE EMPLOYEES

Every contact with potential buyers of your products and services creates an impression that you want to be only favorable. Your competitors may just put anyone on the phone but you should be more selective. Since your customers and prospects will probably never personally meet your telemarketers, looks and appearance won't matter that much. Of course you want cleanliness and personal hygiene to fit in with the rest of your employees. They may have a different dress code than others in your company, especially if they are working in a separate area. Or if they have different hours, like late afternoon and early evening to contact consumers.

People who are successful at telemarketing are a different breed from other employees in several ways. They may not be as punctual and arrive late, as well as want to leave early. They need more breaks and shorter hours so they can be refreshed and ready for each series of calls. But when they're good, your business will see positive growth results. Put them in the right environment, with the right products and target list and how can you not prosper? If telemarketing is right for your business, then the right telemarketer will make you a winner and generate profits.

So, how do you know if your telemarketers and other telephone employees can perform the job necessary to increase sales? Not everyone is cut out for this job and able to perform it successfully. Certain qualities are necessary and you should be looking for them. Keep an eye out for them everywhere you go, and when you find a good possibility give them your business card. Let them know that if they are ever available or looking for a new opportunity to contact you first.

Here are some things to look for when searching for great telephone employees:

- A pleasant and easy-to-listen to phone voice

- Speaking at a speed not too fast or slow

- Proper grammar and correct pronunciation of words

- Do they sound positive and optimistic?

- Are they good listeners?

- Do they speak loudly enough without offending?

- Would you enjoy having a conversation with them?

- Can they be persistent without being pushy?

- Do they know when to stop talking?

- A sense of humor without being silly?

- Are they up on current events?

- Are they friendly and like meeting people?

- Enthusiasm rather than hum-drum?

- Do they sound confident and reassuring?

- Do they believe in your products or services?

- Would you buy from them over the phone?

- No strong accent that is difficult to understand

- Do they enjoy being on the phone?

You may have other things that you're looking for that pertain to your industry. Don't settle for less than you're comfortable with or you'll just have to do it all over again. Do a trial run through of your script or outline and listen to see if they are comfortable doing it. Be sure to interview them in-person and over the phone to get a complete picture, before hiring them. Covering all the issues and questions in the beginning will ensure positive results later. The really good ones will not be easy to find and don't settle for less. Let your competitors hire the ones you turned away.

49

TAKE A SURVEY

If you want to know what your customers are thinking and how they feel about your company, just ask them. Sounds pretty simple, doesn't it? Well, it is. By asking them, you will probably get as many as 80% who will give you the honest answers you need. You are giving customers and even serious prospects a chance to say how they really feel about your business, what products they like, don't like, and want to see in the future. Whether the responses are good or bad, it's information you need to use to improve and be noticed over your competitors. Information drives the business world, and the more you have, the better chance you'll have to succeed in your target market. It's like playing golf; if you don't know what you're doing wrong, how can you get better scores and improve your game? Maybe that's why I take extra golf balls every time I play. Next time I'll take a survey of the others in my foursome and I'm sure I'll get answers.

When trying to survey retail customers, you can even hire an independent firm to come in and do it for you. Or you can have one of your staff walk around and talk to people in your store. Another option is to get a temp who enjoys talking to people to do it for you on a couple different days of the week. The weekday customers may have different opinions than the weekend ones so do your survey during both times. Most people won't want to stop for 15 minutes to respond to a survey, so make it short and sweet. The person doing the survey can just ask people if they will answer three quick questions about your products and services. You could also set up a small coffee & cookies station for them while you are asking the questions. Another idea is to give them a coupon for a common item that they can use *today*. Skip a lot of the small talk and get right to the questions so they can get back to shopping. Three to five minutes is about all the attention that you're going to get.

For business customers, you can do a mailing with up to ten questions that they can do at their leisure. Provide a postage-paid return envelope or ask them to fax it back to you. By keeping the number of survey questions to ten or so you will get a higher response rate. People will not want to take more than 10-12 minutes to do it, if even that long. To entice them to respond you can have a drawing for a desirable prize for all who send the survey back. At the end of your question form you can have a space for comments not covered in the survey questions. Many people will have some opinion about your business and you want to give them the opportunity to express it. Doing a survey like this will show customers that you care about their views and want to improve your business. Direct the survey to the person who places the order for the best response.

Another way to survey customers and prospects is on your website. Have a link to the survey on your home page and encourage people to use it. Again you can offer some type of drawing for people who answer the questions and leave their name and e-mail address. You may also have a way that they can take the survey and remain anonymous if they wish. But those that provide an e-mail address should be put on a mailing list that you can use again in the future. You can also put a note in some of your mailings to let people know about the online survey and the prize drawing. This will keep people that are in your target market interactive with your company. As I have said before, the more information you can receive and learn, the better you will be equipped to fight off all those lurking competitors.

50

SOCIAL SKILLS MATTER

Making customers' and prospects' experience in dealing with you, your associates and employees pleasant and professional is what will make them come back again. A difficult and non-caring attitude may override the product or service that they are buying. Being friendly, helpful, knowledgeable and attentive is the secret to acquiring customers and clients, plus keeping them. We all have to live and work on the same Earth so we might as well get along with each other and make everything run smoother. A candid and responsive demeanor is expected in business and you could put your business at risk if it's not there. If customers dread calling or visiting your company because of how they are dealt with or treated, they may shop elsewhere. And once those competitors of yours show more empathy and understanding you can kiss those customers goodbye for good!

Handling customers and clients with respect and dignity should be a top priority for any owner who wants his business to prosper and grow. A golf buddy and good friend of mine, Bob Dedecker, Sr. Director at P2Energy Solutions in Denver, says that social skills should be taught and monitored at all of your staff levels. He feels that a lasting impression can be created more by how you say something than what you say. Social skills need to be as much of a concern after the sale as during the sale and maybe more so. And when something goes wrong during the course of a project and the client or customer has complaints or comments, let them finish their thoughts before jumping in with a response. How can you give an educated response to a problem or situation if you haven't heard what it is in full? Bob is a good listener and has many situations to deal with at his level every day. Staying cool, even in heated discussions, can give you an advantage and create long term trust.

You need to train and stress to your employees and staff that people like to purchase from friendly companies. And I said friendly, not being a friend. You don't want your staff or yourself to try to be a friend to customers; you just want to be friendly and cordial. If a front line person is having a bad day or has a serious problem outside of work it's best to reassign them to a backup job until their mood changes. If they get into an argument with a customer in person or on the phone they should be relieved immediately and replaced by another staff member. If they can't control how they act and react to customers they should be reassigned, sent home or replaced permanently.

Offering your customers and clients a professional and pleasant source where they make their purchase or buy a service is one way you can stay ahead of competitors. And they will know that if a problem arises during or after their purchase, your company will listen and respond. Not every other business will put in the time and effort to achieve this customer friendly atmosphere. This type of business climate will not only build loyalty but will add value to your product or service.

51

SAMPLES MAKE SALES

If you have a product or service that can really sell itself, then let it do exactly that. Let your potential customer experience it first hand, then stand back and let the product do its own job. You can also see what they are paying a lot of attention to and offer to explain or demonstrate that area further. If you have several levels or models of products, offer to let them sample these *unless* they have already made a buying decision. If your competitor isn't doing this you can be known as the place to *Try Before You Buy*. It also creates a comfort level for the customer and eliminates some of the buyers' remorse later. And there are some products that most people wouldn't buy without a sample or a test run.

Would you even consider buying a $30,000 car without test driving it? Or a new suit or evening dress without trying it on? And ladies, what about a new swimsuit or bikini? Probably not, so why should anyone buy your products before they see, test or handle a sample of them? Letting your potential customer become a little familiar with what you are trying to sell them eliminates most of the problems and surprises after the sale. They will see and experience what they are paying for in advance and know what they will be receiving for their hard-earned money.

If your product has moving parts or does something physical, let the potential customer use or operate it themselves. Don't just show them how it works, let them do it. They can also compare different quality levels and may even decide to upgrade to a better model than they originally planned. The product can sell itself and even convince the buyer to purchase it with hands-on experience. Be sure to point out any benefits that each product level has and let them use it or see it in operation. For large products that can't be operated in a retail or office environment, a video of its operation can also serve as a selling tool. You can even give them a DVD to take with if they can't decide on the spot. That way they can show it to any managers, owners or just get the staff's input.

If you have a restaurant or food service type of business, taste samples also sell. In upscale restaurants, your server may bring out a tray with several different desserts on it to entice you. Your eyes and nose may convince you to order one where just reading them menu won't. When you have a new product to offer on the menu, don't just talk about it, give out small samples. Divide an order into small parts and offer it to people waiting, already seated or over the counter if you are a quick serve store. Some people may even order it right away. Either way, you've got them to at least talk about your item and that's the first step. And you usually see little kiosks or tables in food stores with samples or products you can taste before you buy.

Samples should be a part of every business's marketing mix, especially a small business. If you are in a service business, use photos. Hand them out with a phone number for the prospect to contact satisfied customers. Remember the door-to-door vacuum cleaner salesman who dumped a pile of dirt on the prospect's carpet? No one wants to be a guinea pig, so you have to convince them in advance that they will be satisfied with your product or service. By convincing them in advance, there will be fewer, if any, complaints or returns. That itself will cover the cost of any samples. Remember that satisfied customers tell their friends which creates great referral business. Be street smart and create a happy customer before he buys. The sale will be easier and will generate repeat orders..

52

IT'S ON SALE!

Shoppers love sales; they're getting something they want and paying less for it. We all like the good feeling we get when we save money. It's the *American Way* — a sale! People will buy things they don't really need or don't need right now because of a lower price, but you don't want to have a sale going on for the same merchandise all the time or your regular price will mean nothing. You need to have enough of a margin in your regular price so that when you reduce it, you can still show some profit. You want to be sure that your store is as full of products as possible during a sale, so stock it. An empty store makes the sale look unimportant and will fail to attract passersby. People may think that you are going out-of-business, unless of course, that's the purpose of the sale.

Here are some ideas for planning a successful sale that your competitors may not be doing:

- Choosing a name for our sale will generate interest and curiosity for the customers. Don't just copy a name that a competitor has used, be original.

- Make sure you have enough in stock to satisfy your anticipated demand. People will come to a sale to leave with the product- not a rain check.

- Have the merchandise fit the type of sale. Don't try to sell your leftover swimsuits at a January ski sale or winter holiday decorations at a Memorial Day sale.

- Your price reduction should be at least 25% and as much as 33% to 50% if possible. 10% off is not going to entice anyone to make the special trip to your store or business.

- What you put on sale should be regular items carried in the store that sell for regular price before and after the sale. Popular items work best and will draw people in to see other items that are reduced.

- Have a time limit — *The Sale Ends...* don't let it run forever. People will lose interest after a while and look elsewhere.

- Have big displays of commodity items on sale. It looks like you're expecting a big crowd (which you hope shows up).

- Make sure there are a lot of in-store and window signs about the sale. Hire a costumed character to wave down passing motorists.

- Use newspaper advertising if you can afford it or use an insert with coupons and a map to the store. You can also rent a portable outside street level lighted sign to draw attention.

- Send an announcement to everyone on your mailing list about five to seven days prior to the sale.

- Have the related items together — if dresses are on sale, have accessories at regular price nearby. Or hand tools next to sale-priced power tools.

- Let your customers know of an upcoming sale at the checkout prior to the sale dates. Hand them a flyer announcing the sale and coupons if available.

- If you have a V.I.P. customer list, give them a two or three hour head-start on the sale for the best selection. Do this by invitation only and they'll feel special.

- Talk to suppliers and see if they will give you a better discount for the sale on any larger quantities you may need to stock.

- Ask the manufacturers of your sale items if they will lend you any display items they have to enhance your store's appearance during the sale.

- Tie a sale with something like a holiday or an event happening in your town. Making an event out of your sale may even get you news coverage.

- For end of the season sales, see if suppliers have any left-over related items you can get at a *steal* and add to your sale merchandise.

- If you know for sure that you can't get any more of what's on sale, you can use *While Supplies Last* and display all that's available. Just don't put it on the shelf a month later. People will remember.

Sales are fun, profitable and can bring new and old customers into your store or to your website. If your sale doesn't work, it means that customers didn't value the merchandise at the sale price you set to buy it *now* or even that a competitor was having a better sale than you were. Learn from each sale and the next one will be even better. Study your competitor's sales to get ideas for your own next sale and be a success with customers.

53

DON'T LET PEOPLE WAIT

A small business owner or manager lives for those times when you have more customers than you can handle at one time. People are actually waiting to be your customer. But make their wait too long or even seem too long, and you may lose them. And when you lose them, there's a good chance they won't be back. After you have spent all your marketing dollars to get them in your store, at your website, or on your phone, it's a terrible waste to let them get away. Remember that even one lost customer can also be lost repeat business several times over. So you need a plan to keep them from waiting too long and not being too frustrated when they must be delayed — a plan that you and your employees put into action when a customer is waiting more than is comfortable for most people.

During busy times in a restaurant, most people will not be upset if they have to wait 10 to 15 minutes to be seated. But more than that, and they may become restless and consider leaving. To make the time seem less long, you could put a TV in the waiting area. You could also make some of your most popular appetizers, cut them up small, put toothpicks in them and serve to the people waiting. They will get a taste of something that they usually don't order and will know that you really want to make their wait pleasurable. A few may even order the appetizer, and the profits from their orders should pay for what you gave away. Don't underestimate the power of sampling your products, which also takes the *bite* out of some of the waiting time.

If you own a fast food or fast service type store, speed is always part of the sale. My pet peeve with this type of business during busy times is that all the registers aren't open. The line is long, some registers are unattended, and you see employees standing around talking when they could be helping the people who actually pay them, the customers. I have seen a few places where an employee goes out to the waiting lines with a clipboard and takes an order on a form and gives it to the person in line. When they get up to the front, they hand it to the register person who then keys it in. All the decisions and questions are taken care of in advance, and the line moves faster. If you're in this type of business find a way to move the line faster so *NO ONE WALKS OUT.*

When your business is done by phone, it's very easy for a potential customer to hang up and call one of your competitors. Waiting on the phone always seems longer because you have to just sit there and stay alert for the person to answer. A recording or music on hold can make the time a little less irritating and get rid of that dead silence. You can even have a recording which describes some of your products that callers may not know about. A system like this is only about $400 to $600 installed on a multi-line phone system. It usually includes a four minute recording by a professional radio announcer. Your recording can be changed as often as you like for approximately $75.00 to $100.00. You may even hear people saying after listening to the message, "I didn't know you did that."

People who have to wait to do business with you will only wait for as long as they value your product or services. If there's a way to make their wait less stressful, it's to your benefit to find it and do it. Don't lose even one customer if you can avoid it. Think of all the times when it's not busy and you wish you had that customer. Don't let them get away and go to your competitor. You'll find your efforts rewarded when you see their business in your bottom line. That's where it really counts, so don't hesitate to shorten the wait.

54

PROMOTE WITH GIFT CARDS

Now that we're well into the 2000s (or 21st century) almost any business can and should use gift cards. These are not only for convenience but will promote your business also, if used correctly. The big companies already know this and have been using them since the technology was introduced. They spent many thousands and millions of dollars writing software, inventing terminals, and training employees how to use them. Throw away the paper certificates. A new industry was born and is thriving. And it will keep growing until, of course, something better is found. But today even small companies can use gift cards without all of that expense for software and going it alone in the dark. You will need to use the program available from your merchant services provides (a.k.a. credit card providers) or there are several other independent gift card processing companies that you can use.

The one thing that you definitely want to do is *stop* using paper gift certificates right away. This is because of advanced technology in color copiers and computer graphics programs, duplicates can easily be made and cost you a fortune. If counterfeiters can duplicate our paper money they can certainly do it easier to your gift certificates. Plastic gift cards are safer because they are not activated until they are purchased. Even if some are stolen, they can't be used until recorded, activated and entered in your terminal. The balance is kept in a computer, not on the card. The number or data in the magnetic strip is just a file in the computer records which can be recalled when needed. This is probably more than you wanted to know, but it's much safer than paper certificates.

One of the ways that gift cards can promote your business is by bringing in customers who have never purchased or heard of you before. You only have to get the buyer of the card to give it to someone as a gift and that person will be the shopper at your business. That new person may become a permanent customer and even buy a gift card for another new person. Gift cards can be featured in your advertising and promotional literature as well as on signs around your retail stores. They should also be on small racks at every check out or payment area so that customers can find them easily and be available for impulse buys. Remember that every time you sell a gift card, someone has to come back to your store or go to your website to use it. I'm sure eventually that we will all be able to swipe our credit cards on our own computers to make a purchase. The data will be encrypted and sent to the store or site to make a payment. Small swipe terminals are available now but we need some way to connect them to our computer and the software to make it all work. You can bet that it will be coming soon.

Since all the money on gift cards is never completely used, you can use that statistic to your advantage. Let's say that only 88% to 90% of the value on all the cards you sell is redeemed. That leaves 10% to 12% of *free money* you can use to promote your business and to sell more cards. If 5% pays for the cost of buying the cards the other 7% can be used for discounts. You can offer customers up to 5% off the face value of a card as a holiday sale (you can also set a minimum purchase level like $50 or $100.) Or you can offer another business a bulk discount for buying cards in quantity. It could be someone like a dentist giving a gift card to a new child/patient for the local ice cream store or a financial consultant/advisor giving a family a gift card for a local store. This not only brings you new customers, but it also gives you a free loan in advance of selling your products or services. What other way will people ask you to take their money and say that they will be back someday to select prod-ucts for the money. You know it won't be your competitors or your bank making this offer. Investigate gift cards and find a place for them in your business.

55

SPORTS TICKETS

Most of your male customers and a large majority of your female customers will be sports fans. It's the way many of us escape from our daily grind and problems. We worry about whether our favorite team will win (or beat the point spread) instead of how we'll pay our bills or fix that leaky roof. In some ways it gives us a fresh start, when the game is over, to *tackle* our own goals and situations with a new vigor and enthusiasm. Watching players at the peak of their abilities against others on the opposing team (or one on one) can teach us lessons that life is not so tough after all, even if you don't win every time. So tickets to sports events and games are a good way to reward those larger and loyal customers. It should stay in their memory for months, and even create word-of-mouth praise.

Of course the really big sports events like the Super Bowl, World Series, the Masters, the Final Four or World Cup soccer will be difficult and expensive to get tickets for. You might want to have a drawing for these types of event tickets. Everyone can be included in and have a chance to win them. This is your way to stand out from competitors and have everyone talking about your business. But before you promote this big sports giveaway you must be sure you have legitimate tickets and be positive you have checked them out. You don't want to have your winner or guest turned away at the gate because of counterfeit tickets. It will take a long, long time for your winner and others that they tell about it to forget it. You can be assured that the media would love to get their pencils on that story. I can see the headline now, "Super Bowl ticket winners from *Johnson's Car Service* contest refused entry to the game." Not only will you have to come up with an alternative prize, but you may have to change your name and put all your calls on voice mail.

To be sure your tickets are valid and are good seats use a very reputable ticket broker that has a track record that you can check. Ask other people who have already used them and check the Chamber of Commerce and Better Business Bureau. If you have an advertising agency, they probably know a few that they have worked with before. For an out-of-town game or event, you will need to provide hotel, meals and transportation for the winners. These need to be done well in advance because the big game cities sell hotel rooms out quickly. You may even want to reserve the hotel before you get tickets. It could be cancelled it later if necessary.

If you have a lot of local business or regular consumer customers, you should purchase season tickets to your home town baseball, hockey, football or basketball pro team. If you're in a smaller city, consider minor league teams, college teams, or the nearest big city team. As a season ticket holder you will have a chance at any post season tickets should the team make the championship playoffs. If you have tickets to all the home games for your team, you can make some of them available as employee bonuses or part of a big sales promotion. Many of your customers would love to go to a sports event or game but won't go through the hassle of buying tickets. You do it for them and they will remember you and your business. If the cost is over what you're able to spend, consider partnering with a non-competitor. This way both businesses can be promoted. Share the season tickets and have a cover letter saying, "Compliments of *Hometown Insurance* and *Williams Limo Service*," Actually if you partner with a limo service, they can drive your guests to the game. Be creative and make it fun so that sports tickets will reward loyal customers and generate repeat business. Don't let your competitors be more sports friendly than you are.

56

EXPAND OR NOT?

When your little corner of commerce starts to grow quickly and sometimes almost out of control, do you jump on the bandwagon? Maybe yes, maybe no, or do you just let the overflow business go to your competitors? There are several factors you will need to consider before you take the plunge. And once you decide to chase the demand, can you turn back if you find you made the wrong decision? Remember that if you expand quickly you must have trained associates and employees to work that expansion. Fast growth may be more than you can handle, and if you don't handle it correctly, will it backfire? Well, the answer is yes, if you don't plan correctly.

Let's look at the dot-coms of the late 90s. They hired people like crazy, leased tremendous office space and purchased large volumes of computer equipment until their bubble finally burst. With less income and uncontrolled spending and high fixed expenses, there was no way most of them could stay in business. And all the investors and stockholders went down with them. They thought the wild growth would last forever, and most of us know that's only a fairy tale. Nothing lasts forever, not even you!

So you need to decide if rapid expansion will keep you ahead of competitors or make you just a follower later. Here's some things to weigh and consider when deciding how much to commit, if at all. Just like going in a Jacuzzi, test the water temperature first before you jump in.

- Can you actually profit from rapid growth, and what will you do with the extra profits? If there are any?

- Is it a fad that will just buildup then dwindle, or will it turn into a trend? What are the feasible long term projections?

- How quickly can you gear up to meet the extra demand? Will it be on the down slope when you're ready or still growing?

- Will you need more office, warehouse or manufacturing space? What will you do with this space if demand slows down?

- Do you need more equipment to meet the extra product output? Can this equipment be leased rather than bought?

- Do you have the resources to pay for the extra space, equipment, and people you will need? How much will interest eat into your profits if you have to borrow?

- If you have to hire and train personnel, how long will it take? Can you use seasonal or temporary employees? What about benefits for these new people?

- Will the demand hold as it is now, or will constant product improvements change what the market wants? Can you keep up with these changes?

- What is the marketing and advertising cost to let your target market know you can handle their demand?

- Is your objective to create more profit or to establish a larger position in your market? Are you reasonably sure that you can achieve it?

- Can your competitors move in quicker, cheaper and more profitably than your business? Do they have more re-sources for marketing than you?

- Are you personally sold on the idea of spending time and money to meet the new demand? Are you willing to hon-estly put in the needed effort?

When you answer these questions, you'll get a pretty good feeling of whether you're ready to chase that pot of gold at the end of the rainbow. Talk to your current employees to see if they are as eager as you are to expand. You can't do it by yourself, and you need them in there giving you their extra effort. Are they willing to help you train new people quickly so you don't sacrifice any customer service? Chasing after rapid growth is not for everyone, so think be-fore you make the commitment.

57

SPONSOR A KIDS' SPORTS TEAM

If your target market is local consumers, especially the family sector, you can be one of their favorite businesses. People like companies that are nice to their kids and do things for them. It's a process that creates publicity, loyalty and word-of-mouth advertising. By sponsoring a local sports team for kids you can take some of the expense off the parents' shoulders and maybe even help a child that otherwise couldn't be on the team. When kids are in organized sports, it keeps them busy in their free time and teaches them to be team players. So you're not only promoting your business, but are really helping our future adults be better citizens. It's another one of those win-win situations that you can be a part of and benefit from.

If you can afford to be the team's main sponsor, that's the best for complete exposure at every game and event. You will need to decide what level of team you want to sponsor, such as junior, intermediate, teen/high school, or college level. But the higher you go the more expensive it will be to become the main sponsor. You might want to start low to see what it takes to really sponsor a team and work up from there. You can also talk to sponsors of other teams and get a feeling for the total cost and participation needed.

There are many different sports that kids play such as soccer, baseball, football, hockey, swimming, basketball and probably others. Check the schedule of the sport to be sure it fits your schedule. If you enjoy sponsoring a team and feel that it benefits your business, you can even select two or more for different seasons.

Some of the responsibilities you'll have as a main sponsor will be to provide a large part of the uniform cost and some of the equipment. You might also have to pitch in with the other sponsors for trophies and awards. There will probably be some victory pizza parties and other celebrations that will need to be taken care of. A representative from your company (if not yourself) should be at every game to show support and be sure all promotions for you are being done. I've always been a believer that awards should go to the top winning teams and not last place. Participation awards only reward losers and create followers, not leaders. The uniform should be their reward and encourage them to try again next season. There is nothing wrong with losing if you learn from it and improve the next time.

When you are the main sponsor for a team you will want to draw attention to the games. Having more than just the parents there is important. Use giveaways or prize drawings for those that attend, and entertainment if possible. Try to get stories on the local news and radio talk shows. If there's a playoff at the end of the season, make it an advertised event. Instead of just the championship game, try to get your name into the title game. Or donate a big trophy and call it the *Jones Lumber Cup* or *Taco Heaven Trophy.* Every time the award is mentioned your company name will be heard. The bigger company sponsors do this for all the college bowl games. And don't forget signs and banners all over the field or stadium with your company name on them. Help yourself by helping the kids in sports; we're going to have to rely on them to run the world some day. So help them become leaders and team players.

58

OFFER FIRST CLASS

Many people feel that first class products and services are just not worth the extra cost associated with them. They are satisfied with the regular, medium price, or low price levels and usually purchase those goods and services. The top or premium quality, in their minds, is nice but not for them. A majority of this country's buyers feel this way and that's why the Wal-Marts, K-Marts, Costco and other discount stores prosper. But remember, I said *majority*, not *all*. Some of the buying public feels that they have worked hard and deserve more. This is a market segment your competitors may have ignored.

There is a group of customers out there who are willing to pay the premium price for that extra quality and personal service. If you can provide this above-average product or service and it's accepted, you can also charge a higher price. Some premium things that come to mind are:

- First class airplane seats over coach

- Luxury cars over economy models

- Personal trainer over a gym membership

- Imported champagne rather than a beer

- Lawn maintenance over do-it-yourself

- Complete copy/collating service over in-office copier

- Designer purses over discount handbags

- Fine dining over fast food

- A limo over driving yourself

- Designer clothing over off-the-rack

- Resort suite over a motel room

- State-of-the-art electronics over basic models

- A wedding planner rather than eloping

- Tuxedo-catered event over home-cooked party

- Custom built home over apartment living

- Spa hotel over a motel

- Sports Box seats over grandstand

- Organic food over bargain brands

Personally, I am loyal to one airline for most of my trips because I earn points/miles that can be used to upgrade to business/first class seats. I always feel let down if I have to sit in coach for a flight over an hour. If I don't have enough upgrades, I will purchase them just to get the comfort of moving up. I feel that I work hard and deserve the extra comfort.

You will normally have fewer customers with high-end products and services, but your profits should be more than standard level products. Buyers are going to *price shop* less and look more for the quality level first. But to earn those extra profits, you must provide your customer with the *first class* they expect. If you don't, they won't be back and will likely also spread the word that your claims are not valid. First Class is all that it says, over and above the ordinary, or outstanding. Something that the average buyer is not getting. A feeling of being special or pampered in an ordinary world. If you can provide this in your product line, you will receive a premium price for it. And once your customer believes it, a loyalty bond will also develop.

Almost every industry can provide a first class level if the business owner makes the commitment. But you probably can't be both first class and discount under the same roof. Pick one or the other or have two separate companies. The first class buyers are out there, and you must target them directly. Once you satisfy or exceed their expectations, word will travel quickly to bring in others. Don't disappoint them and keep upgrading what you offer, and the profits can be substantial. A regular first class customer will be a quick sale at a good profit. Once they become loyal, your competitors won't have a chance to lure them away.

59

OUTRAGEOUS COSTUMES/UNIFORMS

Bringing attention to your company in front of your target market and audience is what separates you from your competitors. It makes your potential customers remember you first when the need arises to purchase what you sell. But how do you stand out and keep that image in your prospects' minds, especially if your marketing budget is limited? One way is by your employees' physical appearance which you want to stick in your patrons' mind. In a retail store environment this can be done by uniforms or costumes. Something that is different from what they will see elsewhere. A unique design that sets you apart and also may relate to your products or services. It can be very outrageous or just a little different from the norm.

One thing to consider is the use of bright colors or colors not usually associated with your type of business. But you must be careful not to use colors that would offend your customers or reduce their confidence in you. It's probably not a good idea for an optical center to have its professional opticians wear duck costumes and rabbit ears. But duck costumes might do well for a chain of carwash places. Or bright yellow slacks and shirts may not work for a men's hunting and fishing lodge but may work well for fast food chicken outlets. There are times to be a little silly and other times where it doesn't fit in. Try to match the uniform to the situation and it will be easily remembered.

Some of the best associated uniform/costumes we all know are the colors of McDonald's and the referee shirts of Foot Locker. Somehow even without the business name on them we would still associate them with the business. But if you start using a costume image you must keep using it all the time for it to be effective. A family steak house that has waiters and waitresses wear cowboy outfits on Sunday only won't remind customers of your business nearly as much as if you did it every day. Once you decide on an image, stick with it all the time. It's like an actor staying *in character* any time they are on the set, even when the cameras are off.

If you don't have a uniform or costume now, why not have a contest to let your customers decide what you will use. The prize or prizes can be big discounts off your products or services or even a costume for themselves. It gets everyone involved and their kids will love it. Either give them several choices to choose from or let them come up with something on their own. If there are several people who pick the one you use, have a drawing to determine the prize winner. The ones that don't win get a 10% off certificate toward your products. So use uniforms that will make your competitors stop and say "Why didn't I think of that?"

60

PERK UP SLOW DAYS

Wouldn't it be nice to have one-sixth of your business *every day* Monday thru Saturday? You'd know how many people to staff in your retail store, how many to handle the phones and how much your bank deposit would be every day. Life is tough and business is even tougher so you need to make adjustments along the way. But after you're in business for awhile, you'll get to know the normal times that sales slack off. But if your competitors take two hour lunches or go play golf, on slow days, you can attract a bigger part of the market that is ready to purchase.

Slow periods could be very normal in your type of business. But just because they're a common occurrence doesn't mean you have to enjoy them. Use creative ways to get customers to visit your store or call your business when you need them most. The business owner or manager that just sighs and sits and waits will be the one with lower sales totals. So do something to perk up those slow times, don't just stand there like a deer in the headlights.

Here are some ideas to boost sales on slow days, slow hours and slow months:

- Double/triple coupon values

- Free upgrades to better models

- Free delivery & setup

- Entertainment in store or parking lot

- Free shopper-helper service

- Special sale prices & discounts

- Double points on customer reward cards

- 5% off everything when it's raining

- Gift certificates/cards sent to radio stations that are only usable on slow days.

- Senior citizen discount days

- Have a drawing or giveaway contest

- 10% discount when snow is over two inches

- Do a mailing to regular customers

- A clearance sale starts on a slow day

- Hold a product demonstration or seminar

- Kids eat free with two adult meals

- Special coupons for a slow month

- Have a local celebrity on site

- Have a radio show broadcast from your store

Once you've decided what will work for your business, be sure everyone knows about it. Put signs everywhere including your front door, windows and near cash registers. Send a post card to your customer mailing list with the news. If you take phone orders, announce these offers on your *message on hold* recording. Your competitors might try to play catch up when they see what you're doing, but it may be too late by them. Tell everyone you sell to about the new offers and encourage them to send their friends. You might be the only store crowded when it's snowing!

61

REMEMBERING COUNTS

Do you know who your customers really are, I mean personally? Did you ever take the time to find out, and do you care? Are you as close with them as your competitors are? If you don't know about your competitors, shop their businesses and find out. Most people like to be remembered and spoken to using their name whenever possible. And there are a few, maybe 10% to 15%, that would rather do their business without any personal chit chat, so honor that. But the rest, the majority of your customers, enjoy hearing their name and being remembered for what they purchase. It's always nice to go into a store that you visit regularly and hear, "Hi, Mr. Williams, the usual today?" Or for a business customer, "Good afternoon, Amy. How's the weather in Chicago?" It creates a bond that you just don't have with a first time purchase. It also raises the comfort level of the customer.

So how do you get to this personal level with a customer which makes the purchasing process easier for both sides? You and your staff have to work at it regularly to establish a face-name association. There are books, videos and even classes available to teach you and your employees about name association and also to remember one or two more things about them. If you have out-of-state customers or those who call in or e-mail orders you can have notes in their computer file. You can be just as friendly using e-mail as you can in person. For people you meet in a retail environment you can ask them their name if you see them several times and they also will recognize you or your employees. Then if possible associate a product or service with that name if they purchase the same item(s) often. And don't forget to tell them your name if you're not wearing a badge. People also like to know who they are talking to and will also use your name in conversation.

Some of the best people currently using this type of name association are at your local coffee shop, especially Starbucks. I stop there about 2-3 times a week and many of the people know my name and almost all of them know what I order. It sort of makes me feel good to start my day with a familiar face and hello. Another type of business that not only knows you and all about you is a casino, if you visit often. They know how often you come, what you play, how long you play and what type of payback reward you like. All because of that plastic card you use when you play. But there's no reason why any business, large or small, should not remember their customers by name and what they buy most often. The cost to do this is very little if anything at all.

You can also remember things that your regular customers have done such as a trip they've taken, run a marathon or just changed jobs. Most people will feel sort of special that you even cared enough to remember because many of your competitors probably won't care. And if you can find out when their birthday or anniversary is, keep a record by dates so you can mention it if they stop in during that week. For customers you don't see in person, send a card by mail or e-mail. Showing you care promotes loyalty and keeps patrons coming back.

62

REWARD EMPLOYEES

If you want your customers to experience the most friendly and helpful service when dealing with your company, try thinking *inside-the-box*. Happy and contented employees will always do a better job when providing the service that sets you apart from competitors. Keeping your people comfortable in their positions will show in all their actions and temperament. Many will go beyond what is required and put in that extra effort that makes your business stand out. And when one employee is rewarded it may become contagious as others will want to join in. Happy and satisfied associates work better as a team, so everyone benefits.

So when your employees and associates go that extra mile over and above the required effort in their jobs, they should receive some type of recognition or bonus. When you do this the results will be:

- It shows that you've noticed

- It shows that their effort is appreciated

- It inspires other employees

- It makes the person feel important

But what type of reward should you give them? A cash award is too common, a day off, everybody else does it. Why not do or give something unusual that they will talk about for a long time. Something that they probably wouldn't do or buy for themselves. Here are a few ideas but you can easily come up with many more to fit your situation.

- Tickets to a play or musical — plus a limo

- Pay for a month of their kids gymnastics, karate or ballet lessons

- Pay their phone bill for a month or two

- A full tank of gas and an oil change

- Pay their outstanding parking tickets

- Make their house payment for a month

- Provide in-office chair massages

- Rent a luxury car or Corvette for two weeks

- Toys or gifts for their children

- Have a maid service clean their home

- Buy them a new suit or dress

- Pay for a round of golf for them and a friend

- Feature them in your ads or commercials

- Treat them and their spouse to a full day spa

- Put a lighted sign or billboard outside your building or store with *"Good Job, Barbara"* on it

- Gift cards/certificates for 10 full service car washes

- Create an *employee of the month* special parking space

- Great seats for their favorite sports team

- A gift card or tickets to a big amusement park

- Make a donation, in their name, to their church

Try being a little creative and give them something that's *out-of-the-ordinary* and keep them doing outstanding work for your business. Your customers will see the difference in how they are treated and extra profits will more than pay for these special rewards.

63

USE KIOSKS IN MALLS

Getting your company name and products in front of prospects that might not otherwise see them will bring in some unexpected sales. Everyone you are trying to reach won't read your ads, listen to your commercials, or open your direct mail, so how do you tell them your story? Like a general in battle, hit them from all angles and sides for complete penetration. And if you can reach them in more than one way, all the better. It reminds them of your company and gives them a different look at what you are trying to market to them. Meeting prospects in a different environment shows that you can also be where they can easily find you. Everyone doesn't shop or buy the same way, so the more options you can offer, the more likely you are to entice them to buy from you.

Most people visit their local mall occasionally and some go very often. But rather than pay for retail store space, which can be very high rent and expenses, consider a smaller presence. The majority of large malls (enclosed structures or open) will have temporary space in the aisles that you can rent for short or long term use. The malls will usually have a couple different kinds of kiosks (small, large or on wheels) that may be included or at an additional fee.

These should also be available for longer term rent or on a permanent basis. You will see a lot of them during the end of year holiday season. If you are only going to hand out samples or literature you may get a better price on just using a card table which you can bring yourself. You can set the table up near a high traffic area where many people go by. I would suggest that the person working at kiosk dress appropriately for the type of product or service you are trying to get people to take an interest in. What goes on at the kiosk represents your entire company.

These in-mall marketing stations are great places for a home-based business to get some exposure, especially if your target market is consumers. If you are looking for business customers, it may also work but being there on Saturday or Sunday may be better for business people who are working during the week. Evenings may also work for business to business contacts but weekends should do better if you are on a tight budget. If you have any type of van or delivery vehicle be sure to park it in the lot where your company name can be seen easily, not between other parked cars. It's a free billboard while you're inside (and keep it clean).

Not every business can use this type of selling method but if you can, it will give you exposure that your competitors may not be getting. You will also be able to talk to potential customers in a more casual setting than you would have in a store, office or on the phone. Personal contact can have a bonding effect, especially when you're on neutral turf. If you need a more in-depth conversation with your prospect you can always set up a secondary appointment in a more private location. Having a kiosk in a mall to promote your company gives you a chance to meet people that you otherwise might not see. Use this marketing method if you can and increase exposure to potential customers.

64

CONVENIENT MEETINGS

If you have a home business or very small office and occasionally need to meet with a client, what are your choices? Your first thought might be their office or place of business and that's great if it's available. But if it's not available you will need to find places that give you the privacy, quiet and room necessary to conduct your meeting. Selecting an incorrect or poor site can put a real damper on otherwise successful business relationships. Keeping a professional image by using surroundings that are clean, quiet and convenient can build confidence in you and your business.

Here are some ideas and suggestions for out-of-office meeting sites where you can get down to business.

- If you reside in a gated community, large apartment complex or a large condo development, they may have a meeting room or club house. During normal weekday working hours these are not used much and should be available on short notice. Call the management company and let them know when you're going to use it or reserve it in advance if you have the time.

- For short meetings or when a lot of table space is not needed, try a nice hotel lobby. Most have comfortable chairs and coffee tables that are not being used that often. Be sure to purchase coffee, juice or a soft drink so you are then a customer of the hotel. A light snack or a hors d'oeuvres tray is another option, if it's appropriate for your meeting guest. Don't go during happy hour when it's noisy and crowded.

- Try a restaurant when it's not busy like mid-afternoon or morning. Select the type of food that will best suit your client and where you know the service is great. Some people don't eat meat or other foods so it's best to ask them first. Trying to discuss business during lunch in not a good idea and things may be rushed. Request a table away from other patrons and not too close to the kitchen door or dirty dish trays. Eat lunch first then get to business.

- If you're selling a product that is made or distributed in your local area, you may be able to use their office or conference room for your meeting. Check with them in advance and they may even have a factory rep available if you need them.

- For all of you taxpayers, you can sign up in advance for a small meeting room at most local libraries. Your library card should be the key and there is usually no limit to the number of times you can do this. They do get booked so the more advance time you can plan the better.

- Another idea for short informal meetings (in nice weather) is your local park or river walk. Specify a bench or attraction, statue or street and be there a little early. This is OK for brief discussion or to hand over literature, catalogs and quotations. Exchanging cell phone numbers in advance is a good idea in case the weather turns bad and you need to change the location.

- Another choice would be a friend whose location has a business in the area. If they have an available office or meeting room you can ask the rent it for an hour or two. Just be sure it's a private area and quiet. If they don't take any fee, be sure to buy them lunch or give them a gift.

Meeting with clients face-to-face is important, especially if you're going for that first order, contract or sale. Select the best location and start building that long term business relationship. It gives customers the chance to see the person who they will be paying and always creates a comfort zone. Be a step ahead of competitors and meet your customers in person whenever possible.

65

BE A JUNGLE PLAYER

Whoever said, *"It's a jungle out there"* must have meant retail sales. It can be a ruthless and cutthroat business fighting for the consumer's dollars. It's usually expensive to open a retail store with build out costs, inventory and fixtures, but the rewards are there if you plan and execute correctly. The retail business is fun for some people and a nightmare for others, so you must decide which one you are. When you're having fun, it's always easier to make profits. So if you're going to be a jungle player, do it right and keep ahead of all those other competitive cannibals. They will eat up all your business if you let them.

Many people will open a retail store after being laid off from a corporate position, and want to have more control of their future. These can be abrupt decisions with little or no planning, and that's why the failure rate can be so high. You can be jumping feet first into a market where your competitors have more experience and have already established a position. This is not to say that it won't work and be a success, but you need to plan a strategy. You created a job for yourself by investing much of your life's savings and you want it to pay off. You need to offer the consumer public newer and better products and services, otherwise, why should they buy from you? Should they risk their money and time on an unproven store just because it's *now open* and has an attractive sign? Survival of the fittest will take over and leave the weak swinging on a thin vine.

Getting and keeping retail customers can be compared to chasing a fly around the room; soon after they settle in one spot, they're off again. Retail customers are capricious and fickle; it's just part of the retail business. What they loved yesterday is no longer their first choice today. They might try new stores and respond to new advertising, but if it doesn't measure up right away, they will go back to their old favorite. You want to be that favorite regardless of how big or small you are. The king of the retail jungle has to keep working to stay near the top.

I know a jeweler in our city that never advertises anymore. He only gets new customers by referrals and keeps 90% of his existing customers. He's *not* the lowest price either, but people love his personal attention. I took a ring of mine to him that needed to be made smaller/tighter, and he did it in ten minutes at *no charge*. I didn't even buy this ring from him, although I'd bought several other items in the past. He had the time, and it didn't really cost him much or anything, so he probably made me a long-term customer. He could grow and get bigger with advertising, but he's content the way he is. But other businesses may want to grow and this kind of personal service *at every location* will get them there.

The owner can't always be onsite when these situations come up, but should hire only employees that feel the same. Train them to react the way you would under similar circumstances, and give them the authority to do it. If you like retail, serving customers, hiring and training employees, and sometimes long hours, then put a smile on your face and unlock the front door! If you want to be a player in the retail jungle, keep improving so you keep those hungry cannibals at bay.

~ Barry Thomsen

66

PAY BILLS ON TIME

Standing out from competitors doesn't always mean with your customers only. It means that you are valued by your suppliers as *their* special customer and buyer. Most companies have to buy products to resell, raw materials to manufacture or services to subcontract to their consumers. As a business owner you may also outsource other things, like a call center, manufacturing, distribution, accounting or fulfillment. And to be successful in your target market you need to rely on these suppliers to provide their very best products and services to you and your customers. Most of them won't sell to the end user and will depend on you and your company to support their business. The best way to do that is to pay them as promptly as you can. Your value to them might be the volume you order but how they get paid will play a big part also.

Paying suppliers on time could also help you grow and be more profitable. As my friend and very successful businessman, Roger Aurelio Sr., President of New Supplies Co. in Romesville, Illinois has always told me, pay your suppliers before yourself. Many years ago, when he was building his businesses, he would even borrow from several places to be able to pay suppliers on time. Then

~ 182 ~

when it was time to negotiate the lowest cost on larger orders, he had a little leverage and got their best deal. It's only logical that they didn't want to lose an account that placed larger orders but also paid their invoices on or before they were due. It placed him ahead of other competitors who were also buying from the same supplier.

Many times you can even negotiate prompt pay or early pay discounts from suppliers that reduce your cost even more. A discount of only 1% or 2% allowed to pay early adds up if you are ordering often. If you order from one supplier monthly and take the discount, it's almost like getting 12% to 24% annual return. And if your seller can count on that early payment for every order, you'll get a big A+ on your file. If your cash flow won't let you pay everyone early, select several of your most important suppliers and try to regularly take their discounts if you can. I remember in one of my past businesses a manufacturer had a 5% discount for 10 day payment. This was one that we hated to miss and made our cost of goods much lower than competitors who weren't taking it.

Other reasons for paying suppliers on time or early is to keep your goods coming in when there are any shortages, rations or back orders. Talk to suppliers and tell them if they see a backlog or back order situation coming to let you know in advance so you don't have to wait like all the others. And when problems arise on orders, you should get a quicker response and more sympathetic ear to help solve them. Problems cost everyone money and the sooner they are resolved, the less that is wasted. Also, there may be times when you need a rush order and who is going to help you first; the one who values your business (and payments) the most. It's somewhat like the frequent flyer miles that the airlines use; the ones who fly the most get the little extra perks when needed. So pay early when you can and build some reverse loyalty with your key suppliers.

67

LOCATION MATTERS?

We've all heard the expression, *location, location, location,* but is that a rule that can never be broken? A rule that states that you must have the best location possible regardless of the cost connected with doing it? Well, first of all, I have always thought of it as an expression rather than a rule. And who makes these rules anyways, and what rule book is it in? No one should make rules for your own business except you, because only you are responsible for following them. No one can decide where your business should be located except you. You can seek advice and input but the final decision is always yours, the owner.

Of course, there are certain types of businesses that need high profile locations but others really don't. Your type of business type will determine itself the necessary location it needs to be prosperous. Your competitors will also be looking at a location for their business that will best service customers. Sometimes an average, reasonable priced location that's clean and with a big fancy sign can also work. You only have to pay for the sign once, buy you have to pay the rent every month so check your budget.

Choosing the correct place to open a new business is just as important as any other aspect of the start-up process. When you do it once it's over until you need more space to grow or your lease expires. So don't just jump at the first or second place you see, plan a strategy to get the best available space at the time you're ready to begin or move. Once you sign a lease, begin the internal build-out, and print business cards and literature it will be costly, if not impossible, to change your mind. You may even be able to negotiate a month or two free rent to cover your build-out time. When you collect all the facts that you need to make a location decision, take some time to step back and review everything. You may want to seek other opinions and use them in your decision making process.

When searching your town or city for a space that's going to be your business love nest, don't underestimate the value of a good commercial realtor. The cost of their services to you is usually zero and they can narrow the search down considerably. They have knowledge of spaces that you don't see advertised or on signs. And they can get the advance numbers for rent, demographics and expenses. They will also find out if the landlord is acceptable to your type of business. And, whether there are any competitors nearby and how much parking is available. You make the final judgment, but their help and input can assist you greatly.

After you make the final decision to select your new business location, don't second guess yourself. If you have used all the information and outside opinions, you have to trust your judgment. The chances are that you made the correct decision if you didn't rush into it. It's time to sign the lease, order the equipment for your business and get on with the rest of the process. Once you sign a lease there is no changing you mind anyway, it's done. You will need to trust your decisions in many other aspects of your business so this is a good time to start. Be proud and satisfied with your new location decision and convey that to everyone including your customers. Let your competitors just watch you become successful there.

68

PROTECT YOUR CLIENT

With a service type business, your clients are looking for a skilled person to guide and protect them from making bad decisions. In many cases, they are entering a field that they are not experts in or have never conducted a business transaction in before. Think of going to a different country that speaks another language; you're always cautious at first. And if you can find a great guide, friend or concierge to assist you, the comfort level slowly improves. You will start to feel more relaxed and know that you are being treated fairly for any money you are spending. The same goes for a business transaction, look out for your clients' best interest. When they have the confidence that you really care about protecting their interests and business decisions, it will easily build loyalty and trust. Once you create trust, your competitors won't have any chance of luring your clients away from you and your business.

One of the most important decisions that people make is buying a home, townhouse or condo. It's usually their biggest expense and investment so they don't want to make any mistakes when choosing the correct one. While talking to one of the top real estate brokers in Colorado Springs, Karsten Musaeus of Keller Williams

Realty, I found one of the many things that makes him so successful. He doesn't consider himself a sales person but a consultant, advisor, negotiator, educator and protector of his clients. One of his favorite sayings is, "Tell the naked truth but be dressed while doing it." It made me smile but then I realized that he's right; tell it like it is.

With 30 years experience in residential real estate, he must be doing it right and probably knows many ways that don't work. He said that he won't let a buyer purchase residential real estate if he feels that it's not right for them, even if they are ready to sign the contract. He would rather keep searching for property that will fit their needs and make them happy over the long term. By doing this, he has very few back-outs and very little buyer's remorse. He wants to be available and there for them during 100% of the process plus also after the sale. When the client sees his dedication and caring attitude, they will refer all their friends and relatives to him for his personal service and attention.

Karsten also feels that a deal is not dead just because the two sides can't come to terms right away on an offer. He will spend the time to sit down with the opposing broker and try to work out an agreement that both sides can be comfortable with. Negotiation can save many possible lost transactions and bring them back to life. Why walk away from a possible sale without first trying to narrow the gap between seller and potential buyer. But he also realizes that every situation can't always be resolved and you should then guide your clients in another direction. There will always be another option and not letting your client buy something that is not right for them is the correct thing to do. It will always pay off in the long run.

It doesn't only have to be real estate where you step in and protect your client and/or customer. It can be while you are selling cars, an insurance agent, financial planner or even a lawyer who sees that a lawsuit is a waste of time and money. The "take the money and run" attitude will usually backfire and certainly not build loyalty and trust. If you have been in your field of business for several years, you have a pretty good idea of what is right. Spend the time and effort to protect him from making the wrong decision and you will have people who are truly satisfied after the purchase. Then your referral network will grow much faster than your competitors'.

69

THE TRADE SHOW ADVANTAGE

Attending your industry trade shows regularly is important for any business owner to keep up with current trends and new innovations. You also want to let suppliers know who you are and that you are interested in their products and services. It also gives those factory reps a chance to thank you for your past business. Your competitors will be there so why let them get information that you don't have. If you are limited in time and there is a lot to see you need to have a plan to make it a profitable experience. Making plans in advance will not only save money but less aggravation with the last minute rush.

These are a few ideas to make the most of the time you have.

- Study the show guide you receive in advance and make a list of *must-see* booths and put them in the order of importance. Then work the list.

- Make a secondary list of booths that you would like to see if there is extra time and note their locations.

- Decide what you really want to get out of the show.

Finding new products, new suppliers or just meeting with current suppliers.

- Study the show floor layout so you know where all your *must-see* booths are located and how to get to each one.

- If you see in advance that there is just too much to see in the time you have available, consider bringing a staff member with you to share the load.

- Sign up early for any seminars and presentations that you want to attend to avoid sell-outs. The best ones have limited seating and go fast.

- Try to figure out the amount of time you can allow to each booth and still have time for others you need to visit. Check your watch often to see how you're doing.

- Always pre-register online or by mail and receive your badge or barcode before you go. This will keep you from standing in long lines, especially on the first day of the show. Business casual clothes will usually be the best option.

- Wear comfortable shoes. There's a lot of walking and standing at a trade show.

- Contact your top two or three exhibitors in advance and let them know that you're coming and what you're looking for. If you're already a customer of theirs, you may even get a dinner offer.

- If you stop at a booth and find you have no interest, move along quickly to save time. Smile, say hello and keep moving.

- If a booth you want to visit is very crowded and there is no one available to talk with, consider coming back later. The end of a show day is when booths are the least crowded.

- If you're getting pressed for time, let exhibitors know

that you need only basic information now and can get more details after the show.

- Have exhibitors send literature and samples to you rather than trying to carry it all. Leave room in your carry bag for those giveaways you want.

- Have a lot of business cards with you and hand out freely to everyone you have an interest in. Also give them to people you meet in food areas.

- Drop a business card in all the fishbowl drawings you see. You could get lucky and win a prize.

- Have a pen (or two) handy to make notes on business cards you've picked up or in the show program. It's hard to remember everything.

- Make appointments with any *special* new exhibitors you saw for more dialogue after the show. You both will have more time later for a serious discussion.

- When seated at a table in a concession area, network with other people around you and exchange ideas.

- If staying overnight, see who has a hospitality suite which should replace your need for dinner. And you'll get to meet people in a casual atmosphere.

Remember that your main reason for going to a trade show is to pick up new information about your industry. You may not get another chance at this particular show for another year. You should always come away from a trade show with some new ideas to grow your business and be competitive in your marketplace. If you have smart competitors, they will be there also, so don't let them get more information than you do. Don't just sit on any new ideas or products you find, start using them right away. Let your customers and prospects see your new products, services and ideas right away.

70

THE NEW COMPETITOR

When unexpected or big competition is moving into your selling area, you may need to make some adjustments, especially if you know that they have more resources for advertising, signage and promotion. This is not the time to panic, it's the time to plan. Always check out the *coming soon* banners or just ask the contractors working there who is moving in. The further in advance you know, the more time you have to plan. And that's all you need, a workable plan to not only survive, but to increase your sales and growth. Don't roll your eyes; I've seen it happen many times and it's definitely possible.

Let me start you out on that plan, even if I don't know you or anything about your business. The basic strategy (just like blackjack) works for everyone. You may think you don't know where to start, but just follow a few steps and you, not me, will come up with the plan, A new way of doing business that you should have already been using but you didn't think was necessary to change. But now that you're sort of forced to adjust, it may all be for the better. It may be an opportunity for you to increase business rather than the time to retire.

First, start your plan by making three lists. On List A, put all the products or services that are unique or special and you know that a competitor would have difficulty outselling you. On List B, put all the things that are good selling items but can be purchased elsewhere at competitive prices. You may do a good job promoting these items, but they aren't as unique as those on List A. On List C, put all the things you sell because you think you have to and make very little profit on them. These are items that never create loyalty and customers will buy them anywhere the price is lowest.

Now that you have three lists, let's put them into action. When a new strong competitor is entering your market, it's time to play give and take. Give them all the products on your List C or at least 90% of them. They will probably under price you anyway and there's no advantage in being in a new price war. You're in business to make a profit and List C is not the one to help you do that. Start eliminating them from your store or product line gradually. Your customers probably won't even miss them and you can say that you will be specializing in the items on List A.

Next, go over all the things you have on List A and find ways to make your position even stronger in them. Can you add complimentary items to them or more variety that won't be found elsewhere? Can you become a specialist in these items so no one else will have the in-depth selection? Can you add private label items that can't be found at other businesses? You can even add premium level items at much higher prices because you will get buyers with all different spending levels. You will take over this part of the market and anyone new, large or small, will have difficulty breaking in. This is where you will make most of your profits and create customer loyalty. You can become the expert in this niche market and build trust.

Now let's look at poor List B, stuck in the middle, not knowing which way to go. Many of these products and services may still be good and others marginal. Weed out the marginal ones and eliminate some of them. Pick a couple that, with a little enhancing, can move to List A. Others you may just need to leave alone so you can provide them to customers who have always bought them from you. Price these at a very competitive level and don't expect big profits from them. Competitors may try to under price you on some of these but that's OK. If they are not big ticket products, you should still do fine. And if you're a service type company, you can do the same thing with different lists of services.

You can twist and turn this strategy anyway you want to make it work for you. But by becoming more specialized in the items on List A, you will stand out from the rest of the crowd. Keep looking for more products that you can add to List A that are not available elsewhere. Convince your target customers that you are the place to come to for those specialized items. You will also create word-of-mouth exposure and should expand your loyal customer base. Your new competition will not assume they can push you around easily and price won't be a major factor in the buying decision. You should be able to survive, grow and be profitable against competition in your market.

71

CHECK YOUR NEIGHBORS

When trying to open a new business or grow an existing one, the less problems you have to face, the better. It's difficult enough to do the necessary business tasks and marketing, so you don't want any extra hassles to take up your time. There is also a time to do your homework and diligence when selecting an office or retail space for your business. Asking some key questions and a little observation can save a lot of headaches that you don't need later. Don't rush into leasing or buying your space without first checking some things that can make your job easier or at least less troublesome. Remember the old saying, *"An ounce of prevention is worth a pound of cure."*

In a past business that I was a partner in, we had a noise problem from a business on the other side of one wall. We operated a family ice cream and sandwich shop with a few tables and booths. On the other side of the wall was a business that installed auto stereo units. When they tested them at loud volume it could be heard in our store plus some items even vibrated on the shelves. Of course, we talked to the building owner who met with them several times, but never really solved the problem. We learned quickly to check who our potential neighbors are or will be. Another business location we were looking at for a gourmet coffee store was next to a pet supply store. After watching the area for awhile, we noticed that the pet store let customers bring their pets in the store with them, which is fine for their business. But several pet owners did not have their dogs on leashes and they roamed in the area of the space we were considering. If we had tables outside in good weather, these pets might bother our customers who were trying to relax or read, so we decided against that space. If we had signed a lease too soon, there would be little recourse later.

Years ago I had a sales office in a building that was next to another motivational-type company. Every Tuesday and Friday they had rally meetings with 10 to 20 people yelling and cheering loudly. When we tried to complain we were told that was how they did their business and that they weren't going to change. Since we had a smaller space and paid less rent, the management company did very little for us. So we had to stay off the phones during their hour meeting and moved out when our lease was up. I learned quickly to observe the space before you sign and talk to some of the other neighbors also. What looks like a nice quiet space may have noisy times that you want to know about in advance. If there is any type of government offices in the building you are considering, take note of the amount of people going in and out of it. You don't want a long line blocking the hallway or worse yet, your entrance.

Some other things to check about your neighbors is whether they have a lot of waste and fill up the dumpsters so you can't find room for your trash. Are there certain times of the day or week that their customers or clientele take up most of the parking spaces? You need to be assured that your customers have a place to park and don't drive away and go to your competitors. Also investigate to see that your neighbors are not selling the same products that you are, you don't want a competitor 30 feet away from your business. You can also request that a clause be put in your lease that a similar business won't be allowed in the same strip mall or office while you are there. Check for any odors that might seep into your space from a nearby neighbor. This could sometimes happen if you are next to a restaurant or auto repair shop. But always do your checking *before* your finalize the lease or purchase; it's too late after.

72

DON'T DO THESE THINGS

Both you and competitors say that your own customer service is great and you really care about your patrons. Sure it's easy to say and you may be sincere, but do you know all that's involved in superior customer service? Sometimes it's things that you don't do along with the other things that you do provide that really matter. And all these things can be mental as well as physical. Give your business a quarterly tune-up to see what's really going on and change what's necessary to make you stand out from competitors.

Following are things you don't want happening in your business, if you want to prosper, especially in tough economic times. Many small business owners are not aware that these are even occurring because they fail to check on their customer service people regularly. Copy this list and put it on your calendar and review it at least monthly. If you wait too long, the damage is done and can't be reversed. Once a customer is lost because of poor service or indifference, it's very hard to get them back. These don'ts are simple to correct if you know that they're going on.

- DON'T ever argue with a customer — you can lose 2

ways: the argument and/or the customer.

- DON'T forget to say *Thank You* after each sale or order.

- DON'T ignore anyone who enters your store or business. If you're busy, say that you'll be with them soon.

- DON'T leave anyone on *hold* for more than a minute without checking back with them. If they hang up, you may have lost a customer.

- DON'T treat all customers the same — decide whether they need more or less attention and help. Teach your front line people to adjust to different types of customers.

- DON'T promise things you can't or won't deliver

- DON'T tell a client you will call them back at a certain time and not do it.

- DON'T have business hours to suit yourself — the customer will go elsewhere if you're not available.

- DON'T screen customer service calls, take them all promptly and professionally.

- DON'T underestimate the value of a repeat order. It's your lifeblood.

- DON'T underrate the lifetime value of a customer; do the math.

- DON'T, as a business owner, be too busy to talk to your customer. Make the first contact.

- DON'T answer all your calls with voice mail.

- DON'T allow *front line* people to be rude or discourteous. If they're having a bad day, send them home or reassign them.

- DON'T let your phone ring more than 4 times before you answer it, people won't wait and call someone else.

- DON'T make prospects wait more than 24 hours for price quotes or estimates.

- DON'T close your store or factory so you can go on a vacation (customers may take a trip also).

- DON'T forget to reward regular customers.

- DON'T make customers wait to pay for their purchase longer than is absolutely necessary.

- DON'T wait to solve a problem or make a refund, do it quickly! And fairly!

- DON'T forget to contact customers who you have not heard from in awhile.

- DON'T ignore customer suggestions, welcome them.

- DON'T substitute poor quality and charge for top quality.

- DON'T try to fool your customer or the joke will be on you.

Can you add more of your own? Decide which are the most important for your business and let all your employees know about them. Remind them that without satisfied and repeat customers, no one has a guaranteed job. By eliminating all or most of these *don'ts*, you can also have the best offense against your bigger competitors. What people remember most about a purchase or inquiry is how they were treated. An unpleasant experience will travel to their friends as a *DON'T BUY HERE* rather than a positive referral. Let your competitors have those negative referrals, not you.

73

CONSIDER THE DEALS

When buying for your store, office, or distribution company, you'll occasionally be offered special merchandise at reduced prices. To buy or not to buy-that's the question. Your manufacturer or supplier may have mis-guessed their market and over-produced or over-stocked certain items. They need to turn their inventory into cash so they may offer it at cost or below. It should be very tempting and maybe you can tie it into a special sale or promotion for your customers.

You will have to make the decision as to whether you can move it quickly to your customers without a long shelf life. The price should be great and the sales pitch strong, but don't let that determine your buying decision. It's only a great deal if you can offer it on a special display at a reduced price. They may even have some free display materials they will give you or loan you if you ask them. If you advertise, can you highlight it in your ad? But you must decide if your customers and prospects want to own it. If you can't create interest or there is no perceived need for the product, it doesn't matter how low the price, it won't sell well. If at all possible, try to get a return clause that allows you to return any unsold product for a refund after 60 or 90 days. This may be hard to get because of the low price, but it never hurts to ask the question. But if it's a really good deal you may want to consider buying. You'll also be able to save your customers some money and still make a profit.

Another low risk option for a retailer is selling products on consignment. The retailer receives a supply of products for display or to include in a catalog without paying for them up front. There can be a pre-arranged time period after which the retailer pays only for the number sold and can return or extend the time for the balance. If it's a good seller, you can restock or enlarge the display area. If it's a poor seller, return what's left and you owe nothing more. This is a good method of testing a new or unproven product with little risk. The retailer or cataloger gives up selling space and hopes to get a profitable return. You can't really lose because there is no cash investment going in, only space.

The one risk that you take if you decide no longer to sell the item or items, is a delayed return by a customer. They may bring the item back 60 to 90 days later when you are not stocking it anymore. You may give the refund to keep the customers, but now you're stuck with a couple of the products back. You already paid for them, so you need to resell them again. If damaged, you should be able to get a refund from the original vendor, so put that in your purchase agreement with them. If it's a regular supplier you should get some satisfaction.

Always be on the lookout and be open to special offers, overstocks and deals that you can make quick or extra profits from. There are overruns, deals and overstocks somewhere every day so listen to the sales pitch or have a person on staff to review the offer. You never know when they will come along, so keep a little reserve cash available so you can take advantage of them. Sometimes the unexpected or unusual situations can really add to the bottom line and also put a smile on your customer. After all, you're not only helping yourself but giving a special deal to all your valued customers.

74

INFOMERCIALS & SHOPPING SHOWS

If you have a product or service that would sell on television, you can reach thousands or millions of the people that you are trying to target. TV exposure is certainly not dead, you can tell by all the major companies that are trying to promote their brands. Look at what people pay for a 30 second commercial during the Super Bowl — millions (with an s). Something must be working because it's sold out every year. Not only does big business want to reach the massive audience out there, but they also want to be associated with a quality program. The same logic goes for the Academy Awards, World Series, Emmys, The Masters, Rose Bowl and college basketball's Final Four. Many will also use the phrase *as seen on the Academy Awards*, in other forms of advertising and even on their product packaging. If they are going to pay those outrageous ad prices, they might as well get as much out of it as they can.

But let's be happy that the big guys do spend that money so that we can still enjoy many of our favorite shows. So how can the small or medium size business cash in on all the consumers and business people watching their television at all hours of the day and night? Well, we certainly can't afford those enormous ad fees and may be reaching a bigger audience than we need. The big businesses may be trying to promote their brand but we want to make sales now, not just be on someone's mind. We can look at other television venues that are less expensive and promote sales right away as well as brand retention. These are 24 hour shopping shows and infomercials at off hours or during the graveyard shift. Nowadays you see them all the time so many of them must be working.

A good place to start if you only have one or two products is one of the shopping networks. Many people have built an entire business around selling their products there. Look at many of the stores who are spokespersons for products or have a line of something themselves. They know that there is a proven audience that watches with the intention of buying a product if they like it and how it's presented. So let's all try the shopping show and see how our product sells, right? Well, it's not that easy to just walk in and be on television the next day. There may be 50 slots open during a week for new products and 2000 people who want them. You might have better odds playing poker, but don't give up yet. Most of the shows have a website where you can fill out an application, describe your product, price and profit level and what audience or market it will appeal to. You will either get a form *don't call us* letter or an inquiry to go to step two. They will check out your product and see if it will be profitable and fit on their show. You must also be able to stock their warehouse with enough product for the demand they expect in advance. If you pass all the roadblocks, you should have a good chance to make money.

Another TV venue for a product that has good potential is the infomercial. This is a little more involved than the shopping shows because you do all the work. You'll need to find the time that's available on the network you choose at the time and price you can afford. Sometimes the smaller networks can offer a target market that is more suited for your products. You don't want to be selling a car polish product on the Food Network or ladies undergarments on a sports network. Try to select a network where the audience you're trying to reach watches regularly. Then you will have to film your show for 15, 20 or 30 minutes. The network can usually recommend a production firm that they have used before or maybe even do it themselves. You will also need to hire actors or pitchmen to present your product and a call center to handle all those orders that you expect. The law requires you to ship orders within a reasonable time so you will need a distribution or fulfillment firm to get the product out. Sounds like a lot of work, and it is. But when it's successful the profits will make it all worthwhile.

75

PURSUE LOST CUSTOMERS

No business is perfect and locks in every customer for a lifetime. Things in the market change constantly and a customer's situation can also change. It's rare that every patron will buy from you forever; life just doesn't work that way. So what do you do when you lose a customer? How long does it take you to find out that you lost them? If it's long enough for them to buy from your competitor several times, you're not keeping in contact with them often enough. Many a lost customer, at least half of them, can be won back. Why pass up this extra revenue and profit? Go get them.

First, you need to know why you lost their business. You can't figure out a way to get them back until you know why they left. If you don't know, ask them and you'll likely get the answer. If they say it's because of price, that's probably not the reason, so keep digging. If they have moved out of your selling area and you can't provide products or services to them, that's a dead end. But you can ask for referrals of potential customers they knew before they moved. Ask if you can have a testimonial letter on their letterhead that you can show to new prospects. Your competitors may not be doing this, which is an advantage for you. The worst that can happen is that they say no or don't have the time.

If your lost customer is due to an argument, no matter who won, it needs some time to rest. Back off for a short period that you feel will let the issue jell and be put behind both of you. It will probably never be forgotten, but it can be forgiven. Your first approach should be cautious and not too in depth. A note, small gift or new product literature sent or dropped off can start to break the ice. Let that also jell for a short time before you make that first personal contact. Don't press too hard for new business, just let them know you're there if they need you. Then follow-up periodically until you get them back.

With other lost customers, just ask what you can do to win their business back. They know that you want their business back so don't beat around the bush. When they tell you, pay careful attention to what they say and come up with a solution that fills their needs. Keep a record of what you agreed to do for them and be sure that you do it. Make sure the rest of your staff knows how this customer needs to be treated so there are no mistakes. Another problem or shortfall with the same customer in a short period will probably send them walking, for good. And a solution with one lost customer may also work with another one. It can also be a way of doing business that you can use in your overall selling procedures.

Lost customers are great prospects for renewed business because they already know you and were satisfied at one time. You also know more about them from past experiences, which helps you service them better. It can also teach you and your staff valuable lessons on how to prevent customers from fleeing in the future. Isn't it a good feeling to get an old customer back from a competitor?

76

GADGETS & GIZMOS

There are many ways of being unique in your target market and most of the methods will work for you at least some of the time. Unless it's going to be your logo and trademark, you should change how you visibly stand out from competitors. As soon as you use a gadget or gizmo and others in your field see it working, they will jump in with a similar gizmo of their own. They think that they can confuse the buying public and get some of the market share that you created, which is not all bad if you have another gadget ready in your bag of marketing tricks to counteract them. You saw this in the turn-of-the-century Millionaire quiz show that had a big part in starting the game show reality phase that is still going on today. They use the word *millionaire*, which is a word gadget that gets people's attention.

Gadgets and gizmos can be anything from words, colors, odd shapes, temporary icons to ultra big letters on products or packaging. The title of this book is a gadget because it makes you ask, "What's that?" or "I want to know more." You didn't pass it over, you went to the next step to find out what's really going on here. I remember years back when Kmart used a flashing blue light (blue light special) in their store to announce an unadvertised in-store immediate sale. People would see the light flashing and rush to that area of the store to see what the bargain was. This is a gizmo that worked well because it made people react quickly before the limited quantity or limited time ran out. Being unusual and unique in your choice of gadgets can make you stand out and be remembered in a crowded market of competitors.

Other gadgets might be pagers for a restaurant that call you when your table is ready. This way your customer can go outside and walk around in nice weather. These pager gadgets can also be used for alerting your patrons when their prescription, car service or special order is completed. It can make it more comfortable and less burdensome than standing by a counter or sitting in a waiting room. Or put restaurant menus on hand-held monitors instead of paper. They can be changed easily by computer and everyone will be talking about it. Find something that your competitors aren't using and try it out to see how customers react. Not every idea will work but you could hit on something very popular.

If you decide to use your own gadget or gizmo, then you need to be fully committed to it. It should be the lead in all your advertising and print literature. If it's something that is a fun character, consider having a live person dress up in costume and greet customers or use it in ads. Use it on bags, magnets, T-shirts, and big outside balloons to attract more attention. If you don't know what gizmo to use, have a brainstorm session with your employees and offer a bonus or prize for the idea you use. You can also have a contest for your customers, which is also a gadget to get people involved. If your business is done mostly on the internet, announce your new gizmo or gadget on your home page but show it on all pages so people will remember. Whatever you choose, make it interesting and fun for everyone.

77

HANDLE ANGRY CUSTOMERS

No matter how hard we try to please our customers, we'll have to deal with an angry one at some time. You could hang up on them, walk away, or tell them to leave, but you'll surely lose their business forever. But why not take the other approach and save their business; they're going to buy again from someone. Trying to resolve the situation may not be the easiest way but it's the smartest way. An angry customer who is dealt with correctly and professionally will not only remain a customer, but will send referrals. Here are some ideas on how to handle the situation:

- Let them vent – get it all out so you know what you're dealing with. Don't make any offers or solutions until you know the entire problem or situation. Don't interrupt them, just listen and remember what they are saying. Try to notice if they are stressing one point or repeating it often.

- Apologize for the problem, but don't accept the fault or blame at this point, especially if you weren't there when the problem occurred. Just let them know that it's unfortunate that it happened and you want to do something about it.

- Ask any questions that help you understand what the real problem is. Go over the problem from beginning to end, and learn all the facts. You can't think about how to resolve it if you don't know everything involved. And try not to interrupt them while they are telling you.

- Empathize – show them that you know how they feel and you see their views. Let them know you will try to offer a resolution as quickly as you can. Then work on a solution right away, don't delay.

- Don't argue with them – it will get you nowhere at this point. Regardless of who you think is right or wrong, you want to save them as a customer. Bite your tongue if necessary.

- Thank them for bringing it to your attention – assure them that you're working on the resolution now. If you can't offer an immediate resolution, make sure that you have their contact information. Tell them that you will get back to them within 24 hours, then do it.

- Offer a possible solution and see if it's satisfactory for them or if you can offer two or three choices that they can select from and also something that you can live with.

- Do what you promise and follow up to make sure the customer is satisfied with the final situation. If you delegate the solution, stress that it's to be done cheerfully, and check later to make sure that it was. You don't want the solution to become another problem.

- And if you see or talk to that person in the future, ask again if everything is still OK. This will show that you still remember and care about their past problem.

- Don't get angry yourself, act professional and concerned. It's hard to stay irritated with someone who is trying to

help you. They should back off and let you work on a solution.

These steps won't work in every instance, but should resolve
many situations and save those customers. When you consider the
long-term value of a customer, a little set back now seems insignificant. When you see that customer buying again you will know that
you did the right thing. Once a problem is resolved, discuss it with
your employees so they will know how to handle a similar situation
if it comes up again.

78

DON'T LOSE AN ORDER

I think it's a given that no one wants to lose an order or a sale that you have worked for. Once you feel that you have spent time and effort pursuing a potential customer to buy from you, it has to happen, right? Well, as we all know, it doesn't always happen and for many reasons. But should we hold our ground and demand that the prospect accept our offer, terms and delivery without bending? That attitude will probably lose more orders than it will obtain. Orders and purchases keep any business *in business* and without them the wheels of growth come to a standstill. Without orders you need less customer service, less production and distribution, less accounting and worst of all, less bank deposits. So getting as many of the orders and buyers that you go after should be everyone's goal in your business.

In the roller coaster world of business, we see that good times and bad times fluctuate constantly. A business smart executive, Tom Danza, President of Simplex Corp in Broadview, Illinois never wants to lose an order. Tom says,

"Orders are the medicine for whatever ails you."

When times are good, everybody focuses on cutting costs, staying away from disruptive or "problem" orders. Also, you don't treat customers as well as you should because they have more than you can handle in good times. In bad times, all the cost cutting, focus, etc, doesn't mean anything if you don't have orders. "In good times, even bad managers can look good but in bad times only the best managers look good," This sound reasoning has made Tom's company stronger over the years, and in all economic cycles.

The moral of the story is that you need *all* the orders you can get in good times *and* bad times. One reason is the orders, especially from new customers, will probably become repeat orders in the future if they are handled correctly. So when the times are booming and you're really busy, you should still give that little extra and personal attention. And when you need to negotiate on price, delivery or extra services, do it earnestly, regardless of how much other business you have. If you lose an order to a competitor, you not only lose the repeat order but any referrals that come with it; you lose two ways.

As of this writing, our business is trying to order plastic gift cards for one of our customers on November 12th. The factory normally has 3 week delivery and sometimes faster. We just got a call from our factory representative saying that they can't ship until the first week of January. Well, the customer needs them to sell them before the holiday, not after. We can get them at a different factory for the customer but the cost will be 10% higher. If the first factory lets us take that order to one of their competitors, it's a bad business decision and they won't get any repeat orders. We are trying to find out if they are working weekends to catch up on orders but the higher-up people aren't available. When the end of the year rush is over they will spend money doing mailings and exhibiting at trade shows to get more business. They had new business and let it slip away because they weren't smart enough to figure out a way to fill all the orders.

79

GREEN IS GOOD

The world has selected the word *green* as the symbolic term for ecology and keeping this planet livable. Some people practice it vigorously and others ignore it completely. But almost everyone would like to do his part as long as it doesn't put him out too much. Kids are learning it in school and young adults are really jumping on the bandwagon. I think some have even taken it too far with protests and demonstrations. When you push too hard, other people have tendency to back away and not join the cause, even if they do believe in it. But letting the business world take the first steps and provide the easy path will get more people to connect and link to the *green is good* cause. As a growing business, you can use this concept as a catalyst to stand out from competitors. You can either start this conviction in your industry or join with others in larger organization. But you need to make customers and clients aware of your participation for it to be effective. *Green* is in NOW, so there's no reason to wait.

There may be a couple ways of integrating the *green* concept into your business. You can offer ecology friendly products to your customers, or you can operate your business with all the planet friendly methods. Some of the key words for being green are recycle, conservation, emissions, biodegradable, pollution and organic. If you are just starting to enter the *green* area of business, you may want to start in the easiest areas, recycling and conservation. These are things that everyone can do with little effort. Most areas have regular pick-up of recyclable items or drop-off bins at many locations. How much harder is it to throw a plastic bottle in a box for recycling than the regular trash can? Since plastic is a by-product of oil, you will save two ways; conservation of water and other natural resources will not only be earth-friendly, but will keep prices from rising so quickly.

By practicing the *green* concept, your customers and prospects will notice and may be more inclined to be long term. But if you're doing *green* things in the background you have to let them know. Use signs around your business or store that explain that you recycle, conserve, and don't pollute. Use phrases on your product literature, flyers and advertising. Get the word out in your target market before your competitors do and attract those people who are looking for *green* companies. You may not be aware of who sees your *green* concepts, but they are noticing and they are becoming your customers. Ecology-minded business buyers and consumers also know many others interested in *green* companies, so the word-of-mouth advertising will travel fast. You want to get the reputation for being an ecology minded company before your competitors if you can.

Check with your suppliers to see who has products available which are made with natural or organic ingredients that can be advertised in your business. Also, products made from recycled materials that look and work as well as the processed ones will sell to the *green* purchasers. Not only the dedicated ecology minded buyers will be customers, others will feel some obligation to join in. As long as the quality, price and availability are similar to *non-green* products, there should be no reason why everyone should not be a buyer. Whether it's a feeling of caring or guilt, the green products should sell to everyone.

A few ways that you can adapt for your own business right now are:

- Recycle anything and everything

- Sell and use non-plastic bags and use them over again

- Use low energy fluorescent light bulbs wherever you can

- Sell recycled products as an alternative

- Have a recycle bin near your business

- Use solar power when you can

- Weatherproof and insulate office and factory doors and windows

- Turn the heat and A/C down during non-working hours

Other ways to be a *green* company are to reduce any emissions or pollutants if you manufacture anything. Sure there are government regulations, but why stop there; go beyond and set your own standards. Having your employees car pool is another way of reducing gas consumption and emissions. Buying your own supplies and parts in larger quantities will reduce packaging and transportation waste. Always remember to look for products and suppliers with recyclable packaging, then don't forget to recycle them. Give deductible donations to *green* organizations that you believe in, and, that spread the word. Our children and grandchildren are going to be here longer than we are, so let's leave them a livable environment, even if your competitors are among them.

80

THE BOOMER MARKET

We are entering the era of millions of retiring *Baby Boomers* with disposable money and time on their hands. A lot of them will be leaving the Midwest and Northeast where they had their careers and raised their families and going South or Southwest. They don't want the cold weather and snow, as well as the traffic in their every day routine anymore. Some of the biggest destinations I've read about are Florida, Arizona, New Mexico and southern Nevada/Las Vegas areas, which now opens doors to many business opportunities for smart small companies as well as medium to large ones. *Baby boomers*, who are starting to enter their 60s, will have many needs and wants plus the money to pay for them. Someone smart is going to provide those products and services. Will it be you or your competitors?

One of the secrets to cashing in on the *Boomer boom* is to get there early and be already established when the stampede arrives. Most of them will settle in cities of 50,000 people or more in their destination states. Few will select small towns and rural areas which have limited medical and other services. They will be there to enjoy the rest of their lives, which could be very lengthy. Once the boom starts, it could very well last 15 to 20 years, with new boomers continually entering this segment. Some will not want to work at all while others may seek part-time jobs to fill some of their time and supplement their other income. They will also have a surplus of recreational and fun time available and the dollars to spend on it.

Concentrating on the areas that will be the most in demand will result in the greatest chance for success. Some of those market segments will probably be:

- *Healthcare/medical* – The need for excellent health care never ends and can be even more necessary as we age. Boomers will have Medicare and possibly supplemental plans to pay for the best care.

- *Salons/spas* – Many will now be able to afford and enjoy these semi-luxuries. Have off-hour specials to attract them with soft music and lights.

- *Transportation* – Getting around the city and community in stylish yet affordable transportation will be a need that boomers will use. Free pick-up and rides to shopping centers will be popular.

- *Restaurants* – Non-fast food and ethnic eateries may prosper with this group. Natural and organic foods should thrive, as well as attractive settings and comfortable chairs.

- *Daytime activities* – Local and extended tours or excursions may well become very popular. Longer trips and sightseeing for people their age should also do well.

- *Golf/tennis* – Many baby boomers have taken good care of themselves and can enjoy physical sports for a long time. Provide a place where they can go with their friends and offer memberships.

- *Investment services* – Smart advice will be needed, but they won't be fooled with high charges and fees. Honest, sincere guidance will be a service they will pay for and closely monitor results.

- *Exercise/gyms* – Health clubs that cater to the upper middle age crowd will do very well; places to keep in shape and meet friends.

- *Entertainment* – Plays, musicals, concerts, ballet and movies with special hour pricing can really clean up. Add more matinees for the Boomer crowd.

- *Gaming* – Opportunities for local or mini-casinos with slots and poker can be in high demand. Have low stakes games where they can spend time and have fun.

- *Handyman Services* – Since they may not want to or be able to do home repairs, honest services will be necessary. See if you can you offer a yearly contract for multiple services?

- *Delivery Services* – For all types of businesses, free delivery of products or prescriptions may increase their loyalty to your business.

- *Secure Living* – Buy, build or convert condos and townhouses to gated communities. Offer fair priced security systems for boomer homeowners.

This new group of retiring or semi-retired citizens will want good products and convenience but at a fair price. They will have money to spend but will only spend it wisely and want the most value they can get. Showing them that you care and providing outstanding customer service will create a sincere loyalty for your business. *Baby boomers* are going to be around for a long time and smart small business owners can generate steady profits from them. But if you don't plan now and get started soon, competitors will move in ahead of you. The special products and services that you provide now will also be around when you reach that time in your life.

81

PEOPLE READ NEWSLETTERS

Reading and learning about your industry and related areas should be on every professional's to-do list. Magazines and newspapers along with internet news will keep most people up-to-date on general issues in business and the world. If you don't know what's going on *outside* your industry, you won't have the knowledge necessary to plan *inside* your industry. But company newsletters can be a real asset to customers and suppliers who should be interested in learning all they can from others in their industry. Newsletters can give several different perspectives of products, trends, sales ideas, case studies and even the lighter side of the business you're all involved in. Customers can connect with others through the written word and even share thoughts and questions. By publishing and distributing a newsletter, you are inviting people to become one big happy family.

Newsletters or company bulletins can be either free or paid for. If you decide to charge for your newsletters, make it a reasonable amount so you'll have many subscribers in your industry or genre. I've seen many so-called *sales newsletters* that charged over $100.00 a year come and go quickly. The same goes for the investment industry where most of the information can be found elsewhere at no charge. We have a small business newsletter called the *Idea-Letter*, which is 12 pages and contains no advertising. Our annual subscription rate is under $30.00, with renewal rates even lower. We offer it in print mailed first class or via email at an even lower price. We include articles that I write, new business book excerpts, and articles written by other experts from around the country. I feel that a real newsletter should contain little or no advertising and cram as much information as possible into the pages.

Anyone can easily start a newsletter using his computer and a program that sets up the pages for you. We use Microsoft Publisher, but a number of others will work fine. Then you'll need to decide whether your newsletter will be monthly or quarterly and whether you will provide it free to a specific group or sell it to anyone. It should be at least six pages or more to be really effective and keep people's interest. Try to use some graphics on each page to break up the monotony of just words. If it's free, you will need a list of who you want to distribute it to with their addresses or email. New subscribers to a paid newsletter may want to see some of your back issues, so make them available for a nominal price and print it at the bottom of a page in every issue. You will also need some type of renewal form for them to use when their subscription is nearing the end. We also include industry quotes at the bottom of pages as fillers.

Newsletters can make the editors and publishers look like experts in their fields and increase the comfort level when buying from them. You can even increase that expert level by having a question-and-answer section where you give advice. Encourage your readers to submit items and articles that you publish in future issues. Be sure to include a byline with their name, company and contact information so you make them feel important. Offer free samples freely to get people interested. If your competitors are too preoccupied or lazy to offer a newsletter, you'll look a lot smarter in your customers' eyes.

82

USE IN-HOME SALES

Selling to your customer in their home can still be a thriving business in today's changing economy. It's a great way to get a home-based business off to an inexpensive start. But getting on a level playing field with customers should be your first objective. Many will be on guard in the beginning minutes and you will need to disarm them if you want your best chance to make a sale. It doesn't matter if you are selling aluminum siding, new kitchen cabinets, cosmetics or vacuums; you need your prospect to let down their defenses. Remember, there must have been some interest on their part, or you would not have even been able to get the appointment. So how do you, the intruder in their home, get them to relax and keep an open mind to what you have to say?

You probably have your presentation planned and ready to go, but maybe it's better if you don't just charge right into it. Competitors may just try the hit-n-run approach, but you can have a better chance at a sale if you take a slower approach. Give them some time to absorb your presence; compliment their home, kids and even pets. But don't be nosy and ask personal questions about their life, because that could put them on guard again. You don't want to be their friend, you just want them to relax and concentrate on your sales presentation. The fewer distractions there are in their mind, the more open they will be to what you have to say.

One way to put a family at ease is to give them a small gift. Something for their house, their kids, or even their pet. I always thought that a gift card to a local restaurant or amusement center would be a nice touch. Or something the family could enjoy together like a trip to an ice cream parlor in the area. In many cases, you can make a deal with a local restaurant owner to buy in bulk and get 10% to 20% off your cost. The restaurant will usually realize that you will be sending in new customers as well. In warmer weather, miniature golf course passes work well or movie tickets in the colder months. Whatever it is, you may have put smiles on their faces and closed a little ground on that *stranger* image.

If you're doing a home party for cosmetics, housewares, pet supplies, etc, bring something everyone can enjoy. A get together home presentation party is the time to make everyone feel comfortable and receptive. A dessert is usually what can be shared by all, but don't just bring some off-the-shelf packaged goods, be creative. Go to a bakery or specialty shop and get something unique and different. The few extra dollars you spend could pay off with bigger results later. You should also ask your host to please not serve any alcoholic beverages until the end — unless, of course, you're having a wine demonstration.

When it's time to start your presentation, have your materials and their benefits ready. Keep your mind focused on getting all you have to say out before they can make a negative decision. Of course, if they are ready to buy, stop selling and finalize the order or purchase. Have some type of order form or purchase agreement for them to sign if the products or services are to be delivered at a later time. Once the sale is made, it's best to leave soon so you don't keep talking and reverse their decision.

There are many different types of businesses that can use in-home sales. Don't wait for your competitors to try it first, be an innovator.

The one thing to remember is that you are inside someone's

home, not your office or showroom. This is *their* domain and the best level you can achieve is being a guest. Actually a guest who is there to try to get them to spend some of their money. They also know this and want to be sure they are spending wisely. So respect where you are and you should have a better chance of coming out with a profitable sale and a satisfied customer.

83

VALUE ADDED SERVICES

We've probably all heard this term, but do we really understand what it means? *Value added service* is providing your product or service with *more service.* Something extra, something the customer didn't think they were paying for but they received anyway. Something that makes you stand out from your competitors because they are not doing it. They are not doing it because it's too much trouble, too costly, or because they never thought of it. Some people really want the extras, especially when they first receive them and are willing to be loyal to a business to get them. Value added service can be as simple as a big smile during the purchase or as much as helping a customer assemble something that comes in 50 parts. Or really anything in between that is not usually provided with a similar purchase. If you care about customers and want them to return, find a way to *add* value to what they buy.

When I was a kid, maybe 5 or 6 years old, I did what most kids did in the summer, sold lemonade. The common method was to set up a table in front of your house with the pitcher and glasses and wait (and pray) for customers to come by and purchase some. It could take hours to sell a full pitcher and the better part of a day was gone for a profit of some change. Since Mom was the supplier, there was 100% profit, but a lot of fun time was lost. I decided that I would take a different approach, make more money, offer a better product and outsmart my other grade school competitors. I had my mother make 2 full pitchers, one lemonade and one a Kool-Aid flavor. I put them in my wagon with glasses (and water to wash them) and went a couple of blocks to where new houses were being built.

By late morning the sun was hot and the construction guys needed a cool drink. And there I was with an ice cold drink that was fresh and not watered down. I sold out both pitchers in about 10 minutes and said I would be back tomorrow. They not only got delivery service, but a better product because it was recently made and fresher. I think I charged ten cents a glass (double the going rate of five cents) but price became secondary because of the *value added* service. When I got back to my block, the others were still sitting there with almost full pitchers and the sun was melting the ice. I smiled and waved hello, put my wagon away, and went to play ball with some spending money in my pocket.

As simple and basic as that sounds, no one else was doing it. People love value added service because it happens so rarely and they have learned not to expect it. Competitors may only use price reductions as the extras they provide and make smaller profits. But if you're going to be making the sale anyway, why not make the purchasing experience better, not the price? You might be surprised at how many prefer the extras and pass up the price discounters. It may seem like everyone is chasing the low price, but has anyone ever tried to offer an alternative in your industry? A little creative thought may come up with a *value added* idea you can try to see how many prospects will become regular customers.

Value added ideas can come in many different shapes and sizes. When I was able to upgrade to a better car, I chose a Cadillac (my Dad said I have to buy American, see #2). It was a real shock when I first brought my Cadillac in for service and they offered me a free loaner car for the day and returned mine washed and vacuumed. The higher purchase price didn't seem so bad anymore and I told everyone about my experience. I'm always in a hurry, so those extra things kept me as a customer for many years and still today.

Adding value to your purchase and product can be as simple as free pressing of slacks when brought in for alterations. Printing recipes on the packaging of food items or several different ways of preparing it. Free delivery and set-up for items that competitors aren't doing it for or won't be bothered. And finishing a remodeling or handyman project early *and* within the estimate price. People really want these things and don't expect them anymore. You can surprise them and make them loyal to your business *and* they will tell others.

84

USE TEMPS AND PART-TIMERS

When you have a growing business and especially a new one, your personnel needs are not always clearly defined. But we need to let our customers know that we have enough people on staff to provide the service they expect. Sure, most of us would like to have that extra person or two always on hand, but can we afford them? When you hire a full-time permanent employee, you add a permanent fixed expense. Their paycheck plus employer's taxes and benefits will always be there. Not to mention the cost and time of training and supervision. It's not that easy or comfortable to terminate them if business should slow down. Be sure that when you add a full time employee that you will have a long term sustained need for them.

But what about those peaks and valleys that most small businesses see regularly? Are you just late on deliveries and service or do you actually turn down business? If you're like most business owners, you don't want to lose even one order or service contract. Don't make customers wait longer or get less attention just because you're busier than usual. You will need people to assist when you are busy and not be a burden when you're slow. The best way to do this is to use temps for occasional projects and part-time employees for more regular tasks. Both can be used when there is not a guaranteed amount of work. This will make a more pleasant purchasing experience that customers will not find at your competitors.

One advantage to using temps is that you can add or eliminate them quickly without any negative effect. Once you have found a good temporary agency and a person there who you feel comfortable working with, the process will be easy. They will know the type of person you are satisfied with and can also end the assignment at any time, usually with a moments notice. If a person is sent who you don't like or is not doing what you expect, a simple phone call will replace them the next day. There is no confrontation with the person, and your agency contact takes care of everything. You want to be sure that the temp is treating customers and other employees the way you expect them to.

A part-time person who you employ can be someone you hire for specific days or certain hours when needed. They can be trained to handle specific tasks or as a back up to your other employees and cross-trained. Their hours can be stable or fluctuate according to your needs. They should be flexible in their schedule, which should be discussed during the interview process. Replacing them or downsizing them is a little more difficult, because you have to do it yourself. But when you need them, they are a trained asset to your business. They will provide that extra service that keeps you a step ahead of your competitors.

The cost of a temp will be higher, but there will be no employer taxes or benefits. But the temp agency also needs to make a profit on them. For the convenience of short term and abrupt termination, if necessary, you're paying a premium. For part-time employees, you will be paying a set hourly wage with possible future raises and maybe a few benefits. But if they are flexible in working times that you need, they will be worth it. The part-timers should also be more loyal to your company because they are part of it. The really good ones can also be considered for permanent full-time positions if the need arises. Using temps and part-time employees should give you the adjustable staff you need for a growing business and provide outstanding service that your customers probably won't experience at your competitors.

85

MONITOR YOUR OUTSOURCES

When you can't do all the work, don't want to, or don't have the expertise to do it, a reasonable alternative is to outsource some of it. If you're a small business or home-based business you can't do everything, there's just not enough time. And if you try to, something will suffer and it could be your customer service or marketing. So your next best choice is to outsource some of the things that may be more routine and time consuming. This will free up more time for you to go after new customers and take care of the ones you have. Let the firms that specialize in distribution, fulfillment, accounting, call centers, mailing and hiring do what they do best and help you grow your business.

With all that said, there are some safeguards that need to be put in place when using outsource companies that will insure the results that you want and a smooth relationship. In many cases, these outsource people are having direct contact with your customers and clients. If they are not being cordial and professional, your image will be tarnished. The customer will think that your own employees are working with them or that you selected these outsource people. Either way it's your company, and it's your reputation that's on the line. How can you blame them, they are just trying to make a purchase for a product or service. When a business or store doesn't make a delivery on time, who do you find fault with; the store or the outsource delivery company? Let your competitors destroy their service reputation, not yours.

If you plan to use a call center, distribution or fulfillment company or anyone else that will have direct contact with your valuable customers, check them out, in advance. If you are already using one, when was the last time you monitored their credibility? Or are you just continuing to do your business blindly when it comes to your outsources? Maybe your call center is taking orders for you at the rate of 300 per week and you think that is acceptable and you're making a profit. But what if they are offending or losing another 60 customers a week that hang up before they order? That's 20% more business that you're not getting and you don't even know about it. That extra 20% of business and its profits would probably pay for the call center and put more dollars in your bottom line. Why take the chance of passing these extra sales up, if it's happening? Just think about how much you're paying to make those prospects call you in the first place.

You should be getting reports from your outsources that state the activity and numbers of people or orders they are processing. Meet with your outsource management people and see if you can increase the speed of processing, the number of successful transactions and the courtesy of the people who have contact with your customers. Let them know you will be calling or using them yourself as a periodic test of their ability and friendly attention given to each situation. Then do it or have friends or relatives do it for you. If you are paying big money for a massive direct mail campaign or an infomercial, you don't want to lose even one potential customer. Let your competitors lose 20% of their prospects by not doing their observation of outsources and maybe those customers will be yours.

86

CO-BRAND FOR SUCCESS

Two or more businesses that appeal to the same target market can be grouped together to increase sales and reduce expenses. It's sort of like bundling products together, except you're doing it with an entire business. It can give your customers a one-stop trip to buy different items. And for a home-based business you can make one visit to a customer for more than one sale and service. This can give you an advantage over competitors.

You'll be using one location, with one rent bill, one electric bill, one refuse service and one owner to promote and sell products from two or more brand name businesses. The lower expense advantages are obvious, but the appeal to customers is also a positive factor. Co-branding can be used for two or more franchises or a franchise and your own existing business. Most franchise companies recognize the increased success rate by co-branding that some will even reduce their initial franchise fee (don't forget to ask).

Since co-branding has not been around that long, there may not be as many set rules governing them. It's easier to negotiate deals when each situation can be unique. For a franchise that will be co-branded, have a face to face meeting with franchisors to work out all the details necessary for both sides. Explain what you want to do and ask for ideas and suggestions from the franchise office. You can also consider working with another local entrepreneur whose business works well with yours and start planning new co-branded locations. Using this strategy, you will have more control and less rules and regulations to govern you. You and the other owner can make your own conditions which should be put into a legal agreement. The legal fees to do this will probably be less than any franchise fee would have been anyway.

Co-branding businesses is also a good place to test out a new idea or concept. Since the current or existing business is paying the bills, there is less financial risk trying something new. You can own and operate the entire operation or partner with someone who is just starting out. Either way, there may already be a regular stream of customers that are already a captive audience for your new endeavor. You just want to make sure that you don't cut benefits and services from the existing business and risk losing any of those patrons. You should be adding more, not taking anything away. You might even want to explain (or create a flyer) what you plan to do and how it will offer more advantages and choices than you have now. Tell the customer how they can benefit from using both or all of your brands.

One of the success secrets of co-branding is finding two or more businesses that fit together well. You want to add only brands that will compliment each other, not cannibalize, each other. The goal is more sales, not the same or less. Here are a few ideas of businesses that might work well together:

- Deli (or pizza) and ice cream store

- Shoe repair and clothes alteration

- Florist and candy store

- Roof repair and house painting

- Furniture and appliances and carpet

- Printer and office supplies

- Financial planning and tax services

- Exercise equipment and vitamin store

- Bakery and coffee house

- Convenience store and donut shop

- Quick oil change and tire store

- Handyman services and carpet cleaning

- Camera shop and photo frames

- Travel agent and luggage shop

- Real estate agent and moving company

- Landscaping and exterior house cleaning

- Shoe store and specialty clothes

- Motel and restaurant

- Veterinarian and pet wash

The list goes on to whatever you feel would work well together. What other related products or services do your customers buy? Keep in mind that you want to entice the buyers to purchase from at least one of the brands, if not both or all of them. You can even offer some discount for a second impulse buy while you already have their attention. See if your business or idea can be co-branded and you're on your way to bigger profits with lower or shared expenses. It will be difficult for competitors to lure away customers who are buying from more than one of your brands.

87

SPEAK THE LANGUAGE

In most of the world and certainly in the United States, the universal language is English. If you speak fluent English you can probably do business anywhere. People in other countries will learn at least some English to be able to speak to others from countries they want to do business with. A person from Spain and a person from Italy or Japan may converse in English just because they don't know each other's language. The common ground between them may be English, which is now taught in many countries as a second language. So knowing some English will help many people talk to others in a business atmosphere.

So if you're doing business in the United States, you and your employees should all speak English, right? Well, it's not always the case with certain service employees that have come here from other countries to do work that American workers won't do or accept the low pay for. These include housekeeping people in hotels, restaurant utility people, delivery help and even some people that assist the elderly. You can also find some non-English speaking people stocking shelves in larger stores that can't help you when you question them about finding a certain item. I understand that these people didn't learn English growing up because they came from poorer areas that lacked adequate education. But if they are now working in the United States they should at least learn some basic English and common phrases to interact with customers they might have contact with.

This is where you, as a business owner, can take the initiative and provide better service than your competitors. We all know how frustrating it is when we ask a server's helper in a restaurant for something and they shrug their shoulders and give you an *I don't know what you're saying* look. But this can be corrected to some extent helping your employees learn the basic words and common phrases they might encounter while doing their job. You can have a bilingual expert come to your business regularly and have classes or meetings with the employees that need English assistance. Or you can send them to a local class at a community college or school. To entice them to attend you might offer a bonus or small raise for those that successfully complete the lessons. Most of them will be very proud of themselves and try to give better effort when doing their job.

Your customers will experience a more pleasant buying process where they can get answers when they need them. And your employees should be more loyal to your company because they know that you care about them more than your competitors would. So it's one of those *win-win* situations where your employees *and* your customers benefit. And the third *win* is you and your business, which is providing better quality service which should build a stronger customer bind and longer loyalty that might not be available elsewhere. Don't let non-English speaking employees ignore customers because everyone else is doing it. Be an innovator and change it.

88

FRIENDLY PHONE LINES

As much as email and website ordering has become a part of everyday life, people will still use the telephone to place orders, follow up and ask questions. It's still a more personal way to contact prospects and add that extra pizzazz and emotion that you can't put into an email. With an email the recipient has to read it or can stop it or delete it at any time without anyone knowing. With a phone call, they only have to listen and find it difficult to hang up before you're finished. So don't ignore your phone system because you think there's now a better way. The better way, email, is just another way of making contact and not intended to replace the phone. Leave all the options open and let your customer select the one they want to use.

In many countries, the phone is still the lifeblood of the business because it's the basic mode of communication with customers. Especially in business to business transactions, a phone line can be the connection where the sale is made. So having the right number of lines and other features is important for your sales success. You want to have enough lines, but not too many that it becomes a financial burden. Remember, the phone service you sign up for sends you a bill every month regardless of your sales figures. So make it convenient for your customers and economical for your budget. If competitors have cut back on their phone lines and force customers to use email, you may have a personal advantage by not following them.

Some of the things I've learned about business phones over the years and many businesses are these:

- If you are a retail store, have one or two incoming lines with call waiting. Add another line when it's needed if call waiting is used often.

- If you are an office type business, have calls go to voicemail after a certain number of rings. Don't let it keep ringing if no one can answer it.

- If you are a construction type business, have call forwarding to your cell phone when out of the office, and answer it.

- Have your merchant service and fax use the same line to save money. Seldom will you need both at the same time.

- Buy used phones and equipment from a reputable dealer or on eBay and make sure that you have someone to install the brand you buy.

- Have a back-up power supply and surge protector on your system to keep you connected during severe storms and power fluctuations.

- Have a message or music on hold for the comfort and enjoyment of your callers. Dead air makes the wait seem longer, and they may hang up.

- Don't let anyone get a busy signal during your regular business hours. Get enough lines, call waiting and voice mail, because some won't call back.

- Have dedicated lines for your internet connections. Don't tie up voice lines and delay customers. Ask your phone specialist about broadband and DSL.

- Get to know an independent phone installer and repair person who will be there quickly if you have a problem.

- Buy your phone equipment rather than lease, if possible. Over the long run it will cost less. When you move, the equipment goes with you.

If you take orders, provide customer service, or prospect for new clients by phone, then you don't ever want to be without adequate service. When your phone lines are not operating for an hour or two, you can easily recover. But if they are out for a week or more, you have lost business. Plan ahead and don't let it happen by using call forwarding to phones that are working. Make it easy for clients and customers to receive that personal touch from your business with a friendly phone system.

89

BE AN EXPERT

When you need information or advice on a subject that you know little about or only a basic knowledge of, you look for someone wha may be an expert in that area. They can provide more in-depth information than you have and you will tend to believe them and take their advice. An expert is usually looked up to and if they have a business related to their proficient field, people searching for products or services in that field will be more inclined to buy from them. Being considered an expert has its advantages, both in business and personal satisfaction. It can raise you and your company above competitors because a trust has been established. People will feel that an expert and their business can help them solve problems or provide products and services that are best suited to their needs. Not only will your credibility increase, so will your sales and profits.

So how do you achieve this expert status if you're not already there? If you feel that you already know your field from years of experience and are willing to learn and share even more, expert recognition can be close by. But to be seen as an expert in your field you must be recognized in front of your peers and target market. You need some type of exposure that people will listen to or watch with reference to your field of expertise. Getting acknowledged for what you know and your skills is difficult at best but certainly not impossible. It doesn't usually happen overnight but builds up over time and repeated exposure. Being willing and available to help others in your field can instill confidence in you as someone with expert status. The word can travel to others and maybe someday you might be a household name in relation to your industry.

Some ways to get started on your way to expert status are:

- Write magazine articles for your industry's trade journal or related newsletters. Always file a copy of the printed article for future use or reference.

- Write a book or booklet with new ideas or insights on your industry. Promote the book whenever you are interviewed or in the byline of articles you write.

- Start or participate in a blog that's related to the field you want to be an expert in. Since it's on the internet you will never know who will read it, so be professional at all times.

- Try to get interviewed on the air with local radio or television stations. Send them information on your background and let them know what areas that you feel you're an expert in and can answer questions about.

- Be a speaker at a non-profit organization, a library, chamber of commerce meeting or anywhere you can get ten or more people together.

- Teach a class at a local community college or trade show in your field of expertise. Or conduct seminars at trade shows or even at your business location.

- Be willing to answer questions and help people in your area of expertise.

Being an expert in any field not only can help increase your business, but can give you a feeling of personal achievement. You may get a lot of questions from people, but you will also hear new ideas and innovations in your industry sooner than others will. Let your competitors be your subordinates when it comes to expert status and recognition.

90

AIM FOR BABY BOOMERS

The post WWII generation is one of the most influential buying groups in the market today, and will become even more so in the next 10 to 20 years. Why? Because they have the most available spending budgets. Their children are grown and no longer need support and their savings vehicles are leveling off. They no longer have to penny pinch to get by. They can finally purchase products that they really want, not just settle for. If they want better quality, they can afford it and will buy it. Some smart businesses have noticed this while others have ignored it. Stay ahead of competitors and modify some of your selling techniques to lure this group.

Here are some ways to reach baby boomers:

- Focus on quality and things that will last without constant service or replacement. They want products to work well and not break down.

- Keep it simple and easy to use or operate. Long manuals and instructions will discourage them and they will lose interest.

- Offer security in purchases and any investments that they will be a part of or involved in. Most baby boomers have worked long and hard during their life and don't want anything to be lost now.

- Promote fun things like travel and easy sports. Even if they are still working, they should have more off time to enjoy leisure activities.

- Keep it young and energetic so that "old" doesn't come into play with your products or service. The majority of this group have taken good care of themselves and are not ready for the "old" or "elderly" label.

- Give a high value for the money they are spending rather than *rock bottom prices.* They grew up seeing what real money can buy and won't be fooled by low value.

The baby boomers who grew up on fast food and discount stores are now changing their buying habits and tastes. They may still want fast food, but now they want healthier fast food. A couple of new food stores come to mind that seem to target this group: Whole Foods and Natural Grocers. Their *all natural* claims seem to hit home and they charge premium prices because of it. They even have a few tables set up to eat a quick meal there. I know this first hand because I'm a baby boomer and I shop there a couple of times a week. I do notice that my grocery bill is higher, but I like their products, so *what the heck.* For regular brand name items, I also shop at another chain grocery store, which is also starting to add more organic products.

Even the giant fast food chains are taking some notice and have added salads with low-fat dressings to their menus. Something new is the meal size or side order of fruit offerings which we should all be eating everyday. They don't want to lose their loyal long time customers just because their tastes have changed. If they didn't offer these new items, someone else would and start chipping away at their market share. They spent the money on the research and you can also use it to your benefit. The fact that they are changing things tells you there is a serious reason to do so.

I've also noticed that tanning salons are starting to offer quick spray-on tans rather than laying under those ultraviolet lights for half an hour. Someone finally realized that maybe it's not the best thing for your body. Whether it is or not, the new method gives the same effect without taking the chance and it's much faster. The baby boomers are starting to be the kings of disposable income, so why not find products that they want to purchase. Ignoring their wants and needs means ignoring those extra bottom line dollars. Remember that if you don't go after their needs and wants, your competitors will.

91

USE GOOD LISTS

A big part of growing a business is finding more customers, that's a no-brainer. But with that said, the next question is, *sure, how?* Well, I think you should define the target market or markets you are looking for, then find as many prospects as possible in those markets. Reaching more prospects should always result in more sales outcomes. One of the best ways I have found is to use other people's lists. These seem to pop up when I least expect it but I never overlook them. Or, you can search for directories on the internet and sometimes be pleasantly surprised at what you find. The only limit to finding good prospect lists is your time, creativity and imagination. They are out there and some are even free.

Some of the places I have found usable lists are:

- Forbes/Fortune magazine

- Business Week/Money magazine

- Newspapers (USA Today, WSJ, local)

- Internet stories & articles

- Trade magazines & newsletters

- Trade show guides (exhibitors & attendees)

- Web directories (open directory or Yahoo directory)

- Sales reps customer and prospect lists

- www.referenceusa.com (business & consumer)

When we were promoting magnets and scratch-off games, I found a list of the 100 largest pizza chains in the trade magazine *Pizza Today*. They didn't provide the addresses but did have the websites. We went to each site, clicked on *Contact Us*, got their address and mailed them our literature. We did get two new customers from this within 60 days. I know it's only 2% of the total, but satisfied customers reorder and send referrals. They are customers that we might not have found otherwise.

Another way I have found prospect lists that I have been looking for is through an *Open Directory* Internet search. I was looking for a list of minor league sports teams and just searched *Open Directory Sports* and several categories of sports teams came up to select from (baseball, hockey, lacrosse, etc). We went to each list and chose the teams to market to. You can also just search any word with directory after it and get many choices. They could be lists you won't find anywhere else and they will give you an edge against your competition. So go find those new lists and the new customers that follow.

Once you find new lists that you plan to mail e-mail or call, enter them in your database under a separate file. As you find changes, updates, contact names and new listings, enter them and keep the list up to date. If it proves to be a source of new customers, use it often. If not, delete it and keep looking for other lists that connect you with your target market. Your competitors may think that all this is too much effort and that's good for you.

92

STREET SMART IDEAS

Every business needs a continual flow of new ideas that will keep it competitive in its market and stay one step ahead of competitors. *Street Smart* ideas can be your best because they come from situations that you have experienced in business or learned from watching others. When you get these ideas, great or small, don't just ignore them, write them down or record them. Keep thinking of how you can use them in your business and discuss them with key employees and associates. A new idea is not going to do much good or grow your business if you don't put it to work. They can also put some renewed vigor in your staff because it's something new and innovative.

New ideas that come from everyday observations and experiences can be some of the most productive and profitable ones that you can use. You won't find most of these in business textbooks until after they are in use for some time and the *big guys* already know about them. You will want to find them and implement them early when they can only be used for your advantage. A big corporation takes a long time to implement a new concept while a small business can act much quicker. Look at gift cards, which were really conceived and invented in the late 80s. It took big businesses almost ten years to make them a household product while a smaller company could have been already cashing in for many years. Use your ideas when you get them, don't wait for competitors to beat you to it.

So where do you find these *street smart ideas* to make you a leader of innovation rather than a follower? They are around you all the time, you just need to look. When you visit another business, see what you like about how they do business and what you don't like. It doesn't matter whether it's in your industry or not, good ideas are interchangeable. Also, check out other websites to see what is attractive and informative and use what you like on your own site or in your store or office. Websites can and should be changed and improved constantly so they won't seem stale to regular visitors. Some of the largest corporations in the world never had an original great idea, they just enhanced, improved or did massive promotion of an idea that they found elsewhere.

You may find something at another business that you know you can use yourself. But before you copy it exactly, think about how you can make it even better when you put it into use. What would your clients or customers be excited about after they find out about your new concept or idea? Sometimes you have to *reinvent the wheel* over and over again until it works perfectly. Adding your personal touch to an already good idea can customize it for your business and make it more difficult for your competitors to copy it. Remember, competitors are watching what you do even if you don't see them. Make sure your staff knows that a new idea is confidential until you release it to your market.

So when you see something new working well at a non-competitor's business, ask questions and be nosy. Compliment them and find out as much as you can about it. Most business owners and managers are happy to talk about how they did things if you are friendly and are in a different industry. Be inquisitive but not to the point of annoyance. New ideas that benefit customers, provide better service, reduce costs or increase profits are everywhere. You just need to keep your eyes, ears and mind open to them. And when you find them, use them quickly.

93

PREPARE FOR THE UNPREDICTABLE

Undesirable and unpredictable events can and will happen whether you want them to or not. And as the word dictates, they appear when you least expect them. So since you don't know if they will ever occur or not, why worry about them or prepare at all? Because they will happen to some of us small business owners and/or our competitors, and the faster you can recover the better chance you will have of keeping your business operating and making a quick comeback. So be aware of what could happen and having some idea of what you will do if it does. If competitors are not paying attention and it happened to them, you'll be more likely to survive and get back to normal quicker.

Let's look at some of these unpredictable events that can hold back your business or bring it to a temporary standstill. Maybe they all can't happen where you are located, but some can, so be alert and don't completely disregard them.

- Weather Related — tornadoes, hurricanes, lightning and heavy snow can last from one day to a week. Assess the damage and try to estimate the recovery time. Take photos and file insurance claims for any damage quickly.

- Accidents — chemical spills, train derailments, plane crashes and other events that cause evacuations can be a problem. If you can't get into your business, you can't operate normally.

- Crime Scenes — if your location is the site of a crime, this can tie you up for hours to as much as days. The police and FBI have the authority to rope off any area where they need to conduct an investigation. In high profile crimes, this can be longer than you would expect.

- Employee Injury – minor accidents and injuries may be a part of working, but sometimes a major one can shut down equipment for a lengthy investigation. The EPA may also come in and cause delays, or slow down your business.

- Fires – prevention is the real key here, and don't take it lightly. But if it happens, be quick and get insurance adjusters moving to get a workable settlement. You'll probably have to rebuild or move and find a temporary location.

- The Economy – fluctuations occur every few years and that's normal business. But when the stock market really crashes, it's everyone's concern. People tighten their wallets and your business can suffer big drops in revenue.

- Utility Outages – if your electric or phone service goes out, all your computers and internet connections go with it. It will cut off your communication with customers and prospects. Depending on the severity of the problem, it can take hours or days to correct completely.

- National Disasters – earthquakes and tsunamis can bring much physical damage to the affected area. Again, assess the damage and try to estimate the recovery time and file any claims.

- Volcanoes & Floods – these may occur with little warning, so get out while you can and salvage anything that's movable in the advance time you're given. But don't risk your life or those of employees by waiting too long to get out.

- Man-made Disasters – terrorist attacks like 911 can bring the entire country to a halt, not just your business. Wars can take many military consumers away from you and reduce your customer base. Be vigilant and aware of what's going on.

- Key Employee Leaves – when a person you rely on for years decides to move on, it can leave a huge void that will take a while to fill. Try to arrange in advance at least a month's notice and give some bonus for not walking out early.

- Your Death – this is one that you can't help work out and should have a plan for. Things happen that we can't control and there is no reason why your business should not go on. Your hard working and loyal employees still need to provide for their families and should be able to keep your company prospering.

Being aware of what could possibly happen will get you one step closer to recovery if it does happen. Recovering and getting your business back on its feet faster will give you an advantage over competitors in the same situation. So be conscious of what can happen and be ready to adjust if it does.

94

CHECK YOUR WEBSITE

Most small businesses have websites now because the cost is much more reasonable than it was just five years ago. So everyone and every company has their own site to promote their products and business and some even take online orders. Instead of being a luxury of the past, it's become pretty much a necessity now. You have probably spent a good deal of time giving ideas to your designers during the creation process. When it's finally finished, you send it out to let the world visit it and promote it every way you can. Your new website represents you and your business in cyber space 24/7/365, but that's only the start.

Is your job really over when you finish the design and open it to the public? Hardly; changes must be made regularly and prices (if any) kept up to date. You will need to make adjustments to your home page and also to other link pages. When something new happens in your business or new products are added, get it on your website right away. You really don't know who will be visiting or returning to see *what's new*. And if they don't see what they're looking for (even though you may be able to provide it) they may be gone forever. So keeping it up-to-date and with current products and services is an ongoing task.

On one of our company's sites, I recently noticed that a change of price on an item was not adjusted. Since we are not big enough to have a person assigned to website design, we have to remember to update regularly. While I was checking other pages, I got the feeling that some of the graphics and text were getting a little stale and needed a face lift. We should have done this months ago, but we didn't have an internal system set up. I've since made a note on my calendar every month to review our websites and make any necessary changes. You can also use your computer's reminder service to send yourself an email when it's time to check them out. And if you can't do it yourself, delegate it to someone on your staff, but get it done.

As time goes on, your website may be the first point of contact for new customers and prospects. People will come to browse and see what you're all about *before* making that phone call or sending you an email. So they will assume that what they see will be what they get. If the site is not up to date, they may get the wrong impression and travel on and you will never know. And if you have the wrong prices or they have since increased, trying to convince them to pay more won't be easy. It also lowers their comfort level in buying from you and can cause them to shop around next time. So check your site often to be sure it's up to date before visitors see it. Your website is an important part of your marketing mix, so keep it fresh, innovative and current.

95

HAVE WISH LISTS

There are always things that you want to purchase for your small business that don't fit in your current budget. But occasionally there will be a little extra money left over from a good sales month that can be used for these items which you want or need but are not an emergency. The availability of the money is usually short-lived, so if you don't have an advance plan, it may get spent on non-essentials and be gone. So you need to make a wish list that is ready and waiting for this money to appear — a wish list with things you are ready to buy and the approximate amount they will cost. This will keep your employees happy to know that you are planning for improvements and to replace needed items. Competitors may not be doing this and it makes their employees' jobs more difficult.

Your owner or manager wish list can consist of items that are wearing out or need to be upgraded, things that you will need to buy eventually, but will benefit you if you buy sooner. Some typical items on your wish list might be:

- New fax machine or copier

- Redesigned product sheets or brochures

- Replace some old office furniture
- Part-time employee or temp
- New phone system
- Update your website
- Music and message while on hold
- New exterior signage or face lift
- Upgraded computers or software
- New plants or aquarium
- Newer model postage meter
- Face lift for reception area
- Production or packaging equipment

Another separate wish list you can have is one for your employees. If they can add things that they would like you to purchase, they might work a little harder and smarter to get them. Let them make the list, but keep it sensible and practical (an open bar at lunch should not be on it). Some things on your employee wish list might be:

- New microwave or coffee maker
- Small refrigerator or hot plate
- Planned holiday dinner and/or musical show
- Candy dish or free snacks
- Company supplied soda, iced tea or Gatorade
- Outside picnic table and grill
- Stock the fridge with healthy fruits, etc.
- Television in the break room

- Half day off paid on their birthday

- Employee-of-the-month paid day off

Now that I'm writing this article, I can think of several things to update on our business and employee wish list. It feels so good when you can actually buy or fulfill some of the items. Now all we have to do is find and earn that extra money to use. Excuse me while I get back to work!

96

MAKE A GOOD OFFER

In the retail and restaurant industries, there's a constant battle for new customers. It seems to me that if you took care of your regular patrons better, the need for new ones would be less intense. But regardless of how hard you try, there will be 10% or more that move or find another source. Of course, all businesses need new customers coming in to replace the ones that drift away, and to finance growth. So many of these consumer-type establishments offer some type of sale to entice new faces. And if that sale offer is not good enough, it will be less effective. This defeats the purpose of the entire promotion and the results will show it. If your offer is small compared to the value of the purchase, then competitors will eat you up. Don't allow them the chance to jump in and make your sale or offer look small or insignificant.

I'm looking at a promotional postcard in full color from one of our local fine dining restaurants. It shows a beautiful picture of the dining room and a view of the city outside its vast window overlooking a cliff. On the other side of the postcard is the offer to entice you to want to dine there. But the offer is so restricted and limited that it's not going to work as well as it could. Most couples who can afford this level of dining like to go out on Friday or Saturday evening and this offer says *not valid* those days. The monetary discount offer is equivalent of about 20% off and excludes lobster and king crab. Only one glass of *house* wine is included and no discount on full bottles. With the inflated prices they already have, 20% is hardly a discount. With a discount that low and other restrictions, it might be better to forget the offer and just promote the romantic setting. There isn't much in this offer that entices me to go there – during the week.

This restaurant is not really promoting the best it has to offer: great food, a complete wine cellar, and fine dining when people want it most. After spending a good deal of money on the printing and mailing, the results won't be as good as they should be with a better offer. This meager offer may work a little better at a fast food or family (lower priced) restaurant. There is a chance that it might even offend some regulars and turn off some would bes. The goal of this fine dining restaurant should appeal to people with this level of money to spend when they are most available to come there. Taking away the prime times and limited standard wines with a sub par discount won't attract the clientele they are really looking for. A free glass of wine with dinner would probably work better.

This is just one example of *not* matching the offer to the actual business it should be attracting. You need to remember there are different levels of customers which are motivated by different types of offers. The same offer *will not* work with everyone, so don't waste valuable marketing dollars trying. Decide the exact market you are trying to reach and address your offer to them specifically. And if you have low and high end customers, use a different offer for each group. But make the offer something each target customer will value, or it will be ignored or discarded. Twenty cents off may seem like a lot when buying a pack of gum, but not much at all on the purchase of a hair dryer. Think like your customer and your promotions will show better results. Your competitors will be watching your promotional offer and will use the information to their advantage. Make your offer valuable to your customers and difficult to match by your rivals and the results will be greater.

97

TAKE CALCULATED RISKS

I looked up the word *risk* in the Webster dictionary and it said *'take a chance'*, *'gamble'*, *'leave to luck'*, *'defy danger'* and other similar definitions. Then I looked up calculate and it said *'figure out'*, *'determine by reasoning'*, *'forecast'*, *'compute'*, and so on. So what this way of standing out from competitors is saying is to take a chance on something new but figure out what your outcome odds are in advance. Innovation is always a risk because it's new and different. Many times it will not be accepted in the marketplace, or will be accepted in a different way than first anticipated. Taking calculated risks means trying something that's outside your comfort zone that you have researched in advance. You have an idea for your business that's unique and maybe even unconventional, but you feel it may create new interest in your target market. You will never know if it's going to be successful if you don't try it. And if you wait, your competitors may beat you to it.

This reminds me of a few large company attempts at making changes and taking risks. The one everyone remembers is when Coke decided to change its recipe and sell only the *New Coke*. They discontinued the old formula that had built the company for decades without checking with their customers. The outcry and disapproval was massive and they had to bring back *Classic Coca-Cola* within 90 days or suffer severe sales declines. It was a risk that didn't work initially because they may have done only initial reasoning and forecasting instead of asking the real people who purchased their products. Another risk that did work well was the iPod that Apple invented to replace portable CD players and buying songs and albums in stores. But when they calculated the risk of entering an established market, they targeted young people who were open to new music ideas. I feel that this risk and innovation paid off big because they knew in advance who their customers would be and went after them directly.

These are much bigger companies and innovations than most of us will ever be involved with, but it shows that risks can result in good or bad situations. And even undesirable outcomes can provide powerful information that can be used for your next risk undertaking. Just don't jump into your risk with both feet or you take the chance to lose everything. Test the water slowly at first and move into it when you see that things start going in a positive direction. You may see something new at another business and want to try it at yours. That's great, but before you leap, check out what the results may be. Will it only cost money? That's why it's important to calculate the risk before you take it. Will it put your business in a better position than it was?

One time to take calculated risks is when a big competitor is moving into your market territory. You will usually get some advance notice, which is valuable time to experiment and take some risks that will put your business in an offensive position. If possible, try to visit your new big competitor in a different location or study their website. If they are a public corporation, contact their investor relations department and request their latest annual report. Then come up with ideas and brainstorm with your employees to come up with innovations to try or risk before the new competitor arrives in your market. Remember that risks are not wild gambles if you plan in advance and approach them carefully.

98

THE LIBRARY IS OPEN

If you want to stay ahead of competitors, a good way is to be smarter and have more information than they do. The way to be smarter is to be on the constant lookout for new ideas and data for your business. And if you can get it without cost it's even better. Your best free source of information, open seven days a week, is your local library. Even though your taxes pay for its operation, it's available at no cost when you use it. If you haven't been there lately, I suggest you find some time soon. There's so much information there you can spend an hour just figuring out what to use and look at. Find a comfortable quiet spot and dig in.

You will find directories with hundreds of pages of possible new customers with contact names. The reference department will have information on all the media companies you can use for publicity. If you can't find what you're looking for, a reference librarian will cheerfully guide you in the right direction (tipping not necessary). Most of the books in the reference department are not available for check-out, so bring pen and paper to jot down any details you want to take back to the office with you. If you're checking out books on marketing, sales or any subject don't take just one; take 3 or 4 so you have different ideas from different authors. Then you can decide what will work best for your business. Look for all the options available.

Many libraries have coin-operated copy machines so you can copy full pages of information from reference books that you can't take with you. Bring change or dollar bills so you're prepared if you need to use them. You never know when you're going to find a list of potential customers or ideas in a reference book. And once you find them, you should want to start using them immediately and see if they prove useful.

A lot of libraries in medium and larger cities will have websites where you can go directly to other sites with information the library has a subscription for. If there are publications or websites you would be interested in, but aren't available, make a request to a librarian or write a letter to the executive director. If they get enough requests for the same thing, you just might get it. You could always cheat a little and ask your friends and relatives to help you out and make a similar request. Some of the targeted directories in the reference department cost hundreds of dollars and you can use them at no cost. Don't ignore or overlook this powerful information.

A small business person who's serious about growing their company, should visit the library weekly or at least twice monthly. New books and directories are always coming in along with current editions of existing books. Using every resource available is what the winners do, so use your library — regularly. When you are out of town and have extra time on your hands, stop in a library and pick up some new ideas. There should be no cost or need for a library card to use the books right there. It's certainly better than sitting in a bar or casino, and a lot less expensive, too.

99

WOW! A NEW PRODUCT

One way to stand out from competitors is to find or develop a new unique product that no one else has in your target market. These may come along only a few times in the life of a company and you should take advantage of it as soon as you can. If it's something that needs to be protected with a patent, you can start the process online at *www.uspto.gov* yourself or see a local patent attorney. Once you have filled out the application correctly, you can use the term *patent pending* which offers some protection right away. But before you even get to that step, there are some questions that need to be answered by yourself to see if your new product is really feasible for your market. So without revealing the product to the public, ask yourself and your associates these questions first.

- Are you sure this is an original idea?

- Is there a need that this product will serve?

- Could this product create any problems, damage or harm?

- Will it be easy to explain and/or demonstrate its use?

- Will it be easy for competitors to make a similar product without infringing on your patent?

- Have you done any tests and market research?

- Who will buy this product?

- Can they afford to buy it?

- Will the price be equal to the value or advantages of the product?

- Have buyers in your market been asking for something like this?

- How will you bring it to market?

- Can you afford to bring it to market?

- Will you have immediate competition for this product?

- Should you sell the idea to a larger company?

- Are there limitations to the product that could be solved with more research?

- What type of guarantee will you offer?

- Can you supply enough product if the demand is great?

- How long will it take to *catch on?*

- Are your potential customers consumers or businesses?

- Do you have the resources to create the marketing mix needed to promote it?

- Can you make a profit and how long will it take?

- What are your profit goals and are they realistic?

- What will you do if it doesn't sell?

If you can answer all these questions and are still excited

about your product, maybe you should take the next *BIG* step. Just remember, it might cost you money for a long time before you start making money. Keep a positive attitude and be ready to introduce it to your market. So get started and leave all your competitors in your dust! Good Luck and maybe we'll hear about you in the *Wall Street Journal.*

100

SMART ADVERTISING

For many businesses, especially retail, advertising is an essential part and expense of doing business. It doesn't matter whether it is in the phone directory, newspaper, magazines or online, it must be used to some extent to bring in customers. If you're not doing it properly and your competitors are, they can entice new customers and maybe some of yours. A good marketing mix is important, but some businesses need more advertising than others. You need to spend your ad money where many of your target market prospects will be looking. Quality rather than quantity may prove to be the best bet.

For a small business, the cost of most advertising can take a big chunk out of your budget so wasting any of it is a shame. Not only is advertising expensive, it doesn't always work. There are no guarantees with most media that you will even get a speck of response or profit. They will all sell their heart out getting you to place an ad but can you find them after it's run and brought you no business? It's time to spend those ad dollars wisely and change ideas when it's not working. The media sales reps will try to get you to keep running the ads but they don't have a financial interest in your business.

Try thinking out-of-the-box a little to find new ways to attract new customers. Large corporations use funny or silly commercials just to promote their brand. A small company doesn't have that kind of capital available; it needs to generate some immediate business with its advertising. That doesn't mean that you only can use dull, hum drum ads and never change them. Develop a clever and catchy logo or symbol that will draw people's attention and be easily remembered. Use this symbol in all your ads, literature and packaging. If it catches on, even locally, it will be associated with your company whenever it's seen.

Also look for other ways to promote your business without spending big dollars and test them out. One of the ideas I see a lot of retail stores doing is having people in costumes holding signs by high traffic areas near their business. This can be done during peak hours to attract drivers and get them to stop or come back soon. Many cities have laws that limit the number of in-ground signs that are allowed, but it doesn't seem to apply to people holding them. During good weather, sidewalk sales and grilling food outside will also bring in people who may have just passed you by. Be creative and try ideas that you don't see competitors using. They just might work.

Don't underestimate the power of using the sides and back of your vehicles for advertising. Your phone number or web address should be large, bold and easy to remember. If you only have a car, there are large magnets you can use, allowing you to remove the signs during non-working hours. And the latest thing pizza delivery cars are using is those mini lighted signs that go on the roof outside over the door. When you see one, doesn't it remind you to order a pizza soon? Keep your eyes and ears open and find new ways of advertising without always spending those big media dollars. Use the media only when it works for you, not because you always have. Let your competitors waste money where it doesn't payoff.

101

OFFER PICK-UP AND DELIVERY

All you need is a van or large SUV and you can start this low tech business quickly or make it part of your existing business. There are many busy executives, medical people and home-bound elderly who would be happy to pay a small fee for personal services. You can offer to pick up dry cleaning, clothes for alterations and shoes needing repair – deliver them to the merchant and bring them back when ready. There are three ways to make money from this service that should add up to a worthwhile income. There are very few expenses involved so most of the incoming money will be profit. You will have a few start-up amounts that will be needed, but you should be able to pay them for $2,000 or less.

First, you will need some type of delivery vehicle with a horizontal pole installed for the clothes hangers. If there is more than one delivery person involved, you could use a car for pickups and the van for deliveries. Next, you need to make arrangements with several dry cleaners, shoe repairs and alteration places. Ask for a 10% to 20% discount off their regular prices as a fee for the increased business. Set a schedule for 24 hour turn around and be sure they can meet it. Having merchants in different areas of your town will tell you the target market selling area you can service. You don't want to spend too much time traveling long distances to your merchants and back to your customers.

Next, and maybe the most important, is your initial marketing to get customers. You will need to mail colorful postcards advertising your services to residences and offices in your target market area. You can check the yellow pages for several mailing houses and get quotes from each. They can obtain the lists you need and tell you how many postcards you will need. It's best to purchase and supply the postcards to the mailer yourself, and save his markup. Check with a local or regional area printer (check the online yellow pages) and get several quotes for design and printing. You will want to send them using standard postage which is the lowest cost. The mailing house will certify the addresses and sort to postal requirements. Set a date when you would like them to arrive and your mailer will know when to send them. But don't do it before you have everything else in place and ready to go.

Some other things you'll need for your new business is car size magnets for on-the-street exposure. You can order these from a magnet distributor or your local office supply copy center. I would then suggest putting signs advertising your service in each of the merchants' stores you are using. Then you need a way of answering the calls from customers who need your service. If you don't have someone who can stay by the phone, hire a local answering service to take pickup addresses but make sure they are courteous. You can also offer rush service if you feel you can handle it. Or if you have another business use that phone number and alert your staff. And you can also accept orders by email or set up a regular schedule with repeat customers. The three ways to make money are: the discount from the merchant, the small fee to the customer and those great tips from super service.

102

DREAM BIG

Part of winning in the business game is your own personal drive, ambition and attitude. Keeping your mind focused on goals that are just out of easy reach will place you in front of competitors rather than chasing them. Staying positive when things are not going well will get you closer to success even when it doesn't seem like it. When someone asked Thomas Edison if he had found out how the light bulb worked yet, he said "No, but I know 10,000 ways it doesn't." He was determined to find the answer to the big discovery and eventually he did. But how many others before him and after him gave up and never reached their dream? We'll never know because they didn't keep following their dream and let it get away from them too early.

We all have dreams and goals of what we want to accomplish in our lives, but some of us are afraid to dream too big for the fear of failure along the way. But failure and major setbacks are only training sessions where we learn valuable lessons. How can we know success and fulfillment if we don't have anything to compare it with? Have no fear of failure and you will go further and achieve more in your endeavors. Get excited about your dreams and goals and forge ahead with determined optimism. Some people will reach their dreams sooner than others, but when you finally get there does it matter how long it took? You're there now and that's all that matters.

Everyone says that you should do what you love and money, fame and success will follow. Many times, though, what you love and the next level you need to pursue will be out of your normal comfort zone. So to get to that next level you'll need to step out of your comfy room, throw away your security blanket and maybe even walk on some hot coals. You may even get burned a little along the way, but, hey! That's the cost of success and reaching your dream. If your dream is not big enough, you may have to start over again. Donald Trump has often said; "As long as you're thinking anyway, you might as well think big." If you have a business and want to reach $1 million in sales, forget that and change it to $2 or $3 million. The one million mark will just be a water station on your marathon to a bigger dreams.

During your life and business career, opportunity will knock at your door several times. Don't hesitate and let it walk away. Put your foot in the door so it can't close on you and be gone forever. Don't just wait for new opportunities to come to your door, go looking for them also. Don't be afraid to write down your dreams and look at them periodically to enforce your drive to reach them. Tell the fear of failure to go nag another person because you're not interested. You can have more than one dream, so have several. Once you reach the first one, it will give you the confidence to pursue the others. Dream bigger than your competitors and you will only see them in your rear view mirror.

103

USE THE MEDIA

Using the media; radio, television, magazines and newspapers, can give you and your company wide exposure that you can't get elsewhere. The costly way is to pay for advertising and commercials where you can tell your story your way. The other way is to let the media tell the story their way, with your help. The second method is not only free, but it gives the audience a more non-biased opinion or reference to what you want the public and your target market to see and hear. But you don't just call them up and say you're ready now and how do we start. It would be nice if it were that simple, but it's not. It's not impossible either, you just need something that will interest their audience. Like we said in number 89, being an expert can make you more appealing if your area of expertise is of interest to a broad group of people.

Writing a book or magazine article can cause the media to want to interview you if the subject is appealing to their audience. I've also learned with my last book, *When the Shit Hits the Fan: How to Keep Your Business Afloat for More Than a Year*, that the title can be an attraction also. Although we couldn't use the S__ word on live media we just said, *When the Ssss Hits the Fan*, so that potential buyers could find it easily in bookstores and online. For live TV or video we just covered the *HIT* so we could show the book cover which helps viewers remember it easier. These interviews drew people to the bookstores and to our web sites. They wanted to know more and the media got them to take the next step.

Magazine articles which you are usually not paid for will include a byline where you can describe yourself and your company plus include contact information. If you feel you're an expert in your field, why not share some information with others and maybe get a business contact from it also. It can also lead to interviews on television and radio as well as speaking engagements. The media reaches a lot of people and you never know who might be listening and looking for your type of business. Unless you sign an exclusive contract not to use the article elsewhere, you can contact similar publications to see if they want to publish it also. You can also make copies or include it in mailings. Don't throw any published articles away because you may decide to use them in the future.

Any time you can use the media to draw attention to you or your company, it's really free advertising. And anything that's free and promotes your business in a positive way is a good thing. If you're not a good writer, see if someone on your staff is and have them do it for you. And if you are going to try to get live interviews on radio or TV and haven't done them before, consider joining *Toastmasters International* to brush up on speaking skills. They are a friendly group of people in hundreds of local areas that meet weekly and let you test your communication abilities and conquer the fear of speaking. I'm a member and would recommend it to anyone to learn to converse more effectively. Once you've done a few speaking engagements successfully, you may be in demand for others.

104

HOME BUSINESS SETUP

When starting or growing your home-based business, you need your work area clearly defined and separate from your living and family areas. Find a room or build one in the basement or garage that you can dedicate to your business and nothing else. You need to have an area that's separate (mentally and physically) from your normal living space. Let your kids know this area is off limits to them 24/7. If you're going to have a successful business, you need a professional business location. If your home-based business area is efficient and well laid out you'll be ready to outsmart those competitors you'll run into. And if you use this area *only* for business purposes, you may even get a tax deduction. Check with your accountant for the current guidelines. Here are some things to consider to make your home-based business a success:

- Close off your work/business area in some way from the rest of the house.

- Lock the office door when you're out or during non-business hours.

- Keep children and family members *out* of your business

area.

- Use a modern phone system with multiple lines and *voice mail* when you're busy or out.

- Get *dedicated lines* for your fax and internet (don't have your fax *busy* when on the internet).

- Use the top of two drawer files for your printer, copier and other office equipment.

- Put bookcases on at least two walls all the way to the ceiling.

- Use an L-shape desk for computer, printer, scanner and phone.

- An inexpensive air purifier will clean musty and dirty air from a closed-in room.

- A closed circuit TV system to watch the children and baby if applicable.

- Paint walls a light neutral color to help avoid fatigue.

- Have a separate computer for your business, don't use the family one that should be in a different room.

- Hang motivational posters or pictures on open walls.

- Mount a dry erase or blackboard to keep schedules and appointments in view.

- Keep a clear path to the door for those quick in and out trips.

- Have a smoke alarm and fire extinguisher *in the room.*

- Use a large waste basket that doesn't need to be emptied daily.

- Get a water cooler if you have room so you don't have to keep leaving your office.

- Use a radio or stereo with soft background music but *not* a television.

- Buy a comfortable chair that swivels and rolls

- Have file cabinets that lock for records (and keep it locked during non-business hours).

Many of these things can be purchased used if you are on a tight budget. Make sure they will last at least a couple of years so you don't have to spend time and more money replacing them. Clean and organize your office room regularly during non-business hours. You don't want to spend valuable *customer-contact* time looking for things that are misplaced. Good office organization is the key to quick and effective work habits. Customers and clients won't realize that you are working out of your home if you plan and execute correctly. Make your home-based office a *business-only* room and with hard work and a little luck, your business will outgrow it.

105

THE FINAL CHAPTER

Following are *Ten Marketing Mistakes* that you should be aware of to keep your business going forward and staying ahead of competitors. Read them often and even post them in your office as a reminder.

1. **Trying to outsmart the market** – the market for your products and services will buy when and if it wants to. You can't force buying decisions, you can only persuade or influence. Don't attempt to make customers change their buying habits too quickly, it usually backfires every time. A classic mistake is thinking that you know what's best for them.

2. **Loss of focus** – failure to look at your customer's objectives, rather than your own goals. Your goals will be achieved when you *first* satisfy the customer's wants, desires and needs. Whether you're just starting out, growing, or just trying to survive, don't underestimate the lifetime value of a customer.

3. **Lack of marketing** – when things are going great and your business is growing, you can forget marketing – NOT! Markets, buyers, consumers and the economy are constantly changing. What's great today may need re-thinking tomorrow, so have a plan and work it.

4. **Don't underestimate repeat business** – a growing business thrives on a customer's repeat purchases and orders. Do what's necessary to keep all your best customers and eliminate those that are holding you back. Repeat business costs you little more than great products and customer service.

5. **Poor customer service** – you may have the greatest product or service but if customers are not treated with honesty, promptness and respect, they'll look elsewhere. You need to remind employees that without regular customers, their job is not necessary. Customers will remember *poor* customer service longer than any other thing.

6. **Failure to test** – most small businesses have limited funds for advertising and direct mail. Finding what works best *before* investing a big part of your budget will help you get the most out of it. Do tests on everything and monitor your results and response. When you find something that works well, make the bigger commitment quickly.

7. **Give up on publicity** – if your publicity efforts have not been rewarded, find new ways or turn the job over to a PR firm. Free publicity is available if the approach and timing are correct. But you won't get any if you give up too soon.

8. **Failure to observe competitors** – your competitors are also looking to increase sales and profits, just like you are. If you ignore them and the changes they make, you'll be playing catch-up later. Be alert to all your competition and adjust accordingly.

9. **Failure to change with the market** – what worked last year may need a face-lift this year. Don't get stuck in a rut and let your competition pass you by. The market will change with or without you – jump on!

10. **Not being street smart** – if you can't learn from your failures and successes, you won't achieve the marketing savvy you need to really compete in your market. Street smart lessons are learned by *doing* everyday. Always figure out why something worked or didn't work and make a mental record of it.

Great Success in Your Business and Life!

~ Barry Thomsen

ABOUT THE AUTHOR

BARRY THOMSEN

Barry has written his third book about small business advice from his experiences in owning and operating over 20 of his own. His last book, *When the Shit Hits the Fan: How to Keep Your Business Afloat for More Than a Year,* is available now at bookstores and Amazon.com. All his books are written from first hand experience and not just theory. This will allow readers to learn from his actual street smart knowledge.

Barry started his entrepreneurial career when he was only five years old. He decided that he wasn't going to sit for hours in front of his house and try to sell a pitcher of lemonade. He loaded two pitchers in his wagon and took them to nearby construction sites and sold out in fifteen minutes. When he got back home, his friend's pitchers were still almost full. At age ten, he was given the worst paper route because he was the youngest but he tripled the number of subscribers within a year.

Growing up on the South side of Chicago automatically made you street smart if you wanted a chance at prosperity. To make extra money when he first got married, he sold Amway, Avon and a family portrait program door-to-door. By working on his own, he learned first hand the importance of great customer service. Then working on commission at a computer placement service, he became the No. 2 producer out of 40 people. To learn other types of businesses, he also worked part-time as a bartender at a bowling center, delivered pizzas and rose to assistant manager at a chain pizza store. Next, he worked evenings and weekends at a family owned Italian restaurant where he learned food service and how to handle slow and busy periods.

Now he was ready to take the plunge and try his hand at a business of his own, well almost. With another associate from the placement service, they opened an employment agency of their own as a partnership. After a year or so, Barry wanted more so he started a computer supplies distributorship at the same time. After building extensive mailing lists for both companies, he sold these to other non-competitors and did very well with three businesses going at the same time. Long hours and extra work never bothered him.

As time went on and interests changed, he became an expert in old collectors cookie jars worth hundreds of dollars each for the rare ones. He started buying and selling them nationwide by direct mail (there was no eBay then). Next, he started a business forms company in the mid 1980s which grew to over three million in sales after 14 years. During those years, he also became a collector and seller of old rare casino chips and authentic hand-signed Norman Rockwell lithographs. He bought and sold enough of these to purchase a second home in Colorado where he now lives.

As more years passed and more knowledge gained, he became a partner in a retail ice cream store and sold decorative Asian items at an antique mall. Then he started his current business which sells plastic cards, scratch cards and promotional items. During those past years, he advised and helped many other small business people with start-up and other ideas to grow. He found he got a lot of personal satisfaction from helping others so he started a monthly newsletter called the Idea-Letter which has subscribers nationwide. He also started writing small business articles, many of which are published in magazines, newspapers and on the AMA website.

Barry decided to write a book or two to share all the good and bad experiences he has encountered along the way. He knew that the life of a small business person was not all fun and profits, but sometimes problems and even disasters. He loves small business and even though the road has been rocky at times, he wouldn't have it any other way – the *street smart* way.

THE IDEA-LETTER

For a *free* sample of our small business newsletter go to
www.idealetter.com
or call us at 877.700.1322.